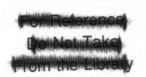

Biography Today

Profiles of People of Interest to Young Readers

Today

Sports

Volume 13

Cherie D. Abbey
Managing Editor

Kevin Hillstrom
Editor

615 Griswold Street • Detroit, Michigan 48226

Omnigraphics, Inc.

Cherie D. Abbey, *Managing Editor*
Kevin Hillstrom, *Editor*

Laurie Hillstrom, *Sketch Writer*

Allison A. Beckett, Mary Butler, and Linda Strand, *Research Staff*

* * *

Peter E. Ruffner, *Publisher*
Frederick G. Ruffner, Jr., *Chairman*
Matthew P. Barbour, *Senior Vice President*
Kay Gill, *Vice President — Directories*

* * *

Elizabeth Barbour, *Research and Permissions Coordinator*
David P. Bianco, *Marketing Director*
Leif A. Gruenberg, *Development Manager*
Kevin Hayes, *Operations Manager*
Barry Puckett, *Librarian*
Cherry Stockdale, *Permissions Assistant*

Shirley Amore, Don Brown, John L. Chetcuti, Kevin Glover,
Martha Johns, and Kirk Kauffman, *Administrative Staff*

The information in this publication was compiled from the sources cited and from other sources considered reliable. While every possible effort has been made to ensure reliability, the publisher will not assume liability for damages caused by inaccuracies in the data, and makes no warranty, express or implied, on the accuracy of the information contained herein.

This book is printed on acid-free paper meeting the ANSI Z39.48 Standard. The infinity symbol that appears above indicates that the paper in this book meets that standard.

Printed in the United States

Contents

Preface

Welcome to the 13th volume of the **Biography Today Sports** series. We are publishing this series in response to suggestions from our readers, who want more coverage of more people in *Biography Today*. Several volumes, covering **Artists, Authors, Business Leaders, Performing Artists, Scientists and Inventors, Sports Figures,** and **World Leaders,** have appeared thus far in the Subject Series. Each of these hardcover volumes is 200 pages in length and covers approximately 10 individuals of interest to readers ages 9 and above. The length and format of the entries are like those found in the regular issues of *Biography Today*, but there is **no duplication** between the regular series and the special subject volumes.

The Plan of the Work

As with the regular issues of *Biography Today*, this special subject volume on **Sports** was especially created to appeal to young readers in a format they can enjoy reading and readily understand. Each volume contains alphabetically arranged sketches. Each entry provides at least one picture of the individual profiled, and bold-faced rubrics lead the reader to information on birth, youth, early memories, education, first jobs, marriage and family, career highlights, memorable experiences, hobbies, and honors and awards. Each of the entries ends with a list of easily accessible sources designed to lead the student to further reading on the individual and a current address. Obituary entries are also included, written to provide a perspective on the individual's entire career. Obituaries are clearly marked in both the table of contents and at the beginning of the entry.

Biographies are prepared by Omnigraphics editors after extensive research, utilizing the most current materials available. Those sources that are generally available to students appear in the list of further reading at the end of the sketch.

Indexes

Cumulative indexes are an important component of *Biography Today*. Each issue of the *Biography Today* Subject Series includes a **Cumulative General Index**, which comprises all individuals profiled in *Biography Today* since the series began in 1992. The names appear in bold faced type, followed by the issue in which they appeared. The Cumulative General Index also contains the occupations, nationalities, and ethnic and minority origins of individuals profiled. In addition, we compile three other indexes: Names Index, Places of Birth Index, and Birthday Index. These three indexes are featured on our web site, www.biographytoday.com. All *Biography Today* indexes are cumulative, including all individuals profiled in both the General Series and the Subject Series.

Our Advisors

This series was reviewed by an Advisory Board comprised of librarians, children's literature specialists, and reading instructors to ensure that the concept of this publication—to provide a readable and accessible biographical magazine for young readers—was on target. They evaluated the title as it developed, and their suggestions have proved invaluable. Any errors, however, are ours alone. We'd like to list the Advisory Board members, and to thank them for their efforts.

Gail Beaver
Adjunct Lecturer
University of Michigan
Ann Arbor, MI

Cindy Cares
Youth Services Librarian
Southfield Public Library
Southfield, MI

Carol A. Doll
School of Information Science and Policy
University of Albany, SUNY
Albany, NY

Kathleen Hayes-Parvin
Language Arts Teacher
Birney Middle School
Southfield, MI

Karen Imarisio
Assistant Head of Adult Services
Bloomfield Twp. Public Library
Bloomfield Hills, MI

Rosemary Orlando
Director
St. Clair Shores Public Library
St. Clair Shores, MI

Our Advisory Board stressed to us that we should not shy away from controversial or unconventional people in our profiles, and we have tried to follow their advice. The Advisory Board also mentioned that the sketches might be useful in reluctant reader and adult literacy programs, and we would value any comments librarians might have about the suitability of our magazine for those purposes.

Your Comments Are Welcome

Our goal is to be accurate and up-to-date, to give young readers information they can learn from and enjoy. Now we want to know what you think. Take a look at this issue of *Biography Today*, on approval. Write or call me with your comments. We want to provide an excellent source of biographical information for young people. Let us know how you think we're doing.

Cherie Abbey
Managing Editor, *Biography Today*
Omnigraphics, Inc.
615 Griswold Street
Detroit, MI 48226

editor@biographytoday.com
www.biographytoday.com

Gretchen Bleiler 1981-

American Snowboarder
Winner of Gold Medals in Women's Halfpipe at the
2005 Winter X Games, Gravity Games, and U.S. Open
Snowboard Championships

BIRTH AND YOUTH

Gretchen Bleiler was born on April 10, 1981, in Toledo, Ohio. Influenced by the example of her three older brothers, she started playing sports at the age of four. She excelled at swimming and diving as a girl and always dreamed of someday competing in the Olympic Games. When Gretchen was 10, her family moved to Aspen, Colorado—a town in the Rocky Mountains that is home to one of the top ski resorts in the United States. After moving to Aspen Gretchen took up ice hockey, hoping to make it to the Olympics in that sport.

During her junior year of high school, however, Gretchen discovered snowboarding. She proved to be a natural in this new sport, which had just made its Olympic debut at the 1998 Games in Nagano, Japan. Snowboarding allowed Gretchen to use the twists, flips, and aerial body control she had learned in diving, as well as the balance, edge control, and aggressiveness she had developed in hockey. She initially competed in all of the major snowboarding contests—including halfpipe, freestyle, and slalom events—but during her senior year she began to specialize in the halfpipe.

> **"I had always expected to go right to college, but snowboarding changed that,"** Bleiler explained. **"I had a lot of hope and drive and wanted to see how far my snowboarding would go. . . . It's a different kind of education than college, but I think it's an equal one."**

In a snowboarding halfpipe competition, riders glide back and forth across a giant U-shaped tube of snow. They gather speed on the downward slope, then perform high-flying aerial tricks at the top of the upward slope. A team of judges evaluates each rider's amplitude (height above the top of the pipe), smoothness (success in linking tricks together), and degree of difficulty, awarding a numerical score on a 50.0-point scale. All competitors make two qualifying runs, after which the top scorers advance to the finals. The finals consist of two more runs, and the top three riders earn spots on the podium.

EDUCATION

Bleiler attended Aspen High School. She joined the snowboard team during her junior year and made it all the way to the national championships during her first season of competition. As a senior, she traveled all over the country to participate in snowboarding contests. Luckily, she had worked hard during her first three years of high school and completed most of her academic requirements, so she still graduated on schedule in 1999. She was selected for the U.S. National Snowboard Team straight out of high school.

Bleiler performs a jump at the halfpipe competition at the 2002 World Cup.

Although Bleiler was accepted to both the University of Colorado and Colorado College, she chose to defer admission in order to pursue snowboarding. "I had always expected to go right to college, but snowboarding changed that," she explained. "I had a lot of hope and drive and wanted to see how far my snowboarding would go. . . . It's a different kind of education than college, but I think it's an equal one."

CAREER HIGHLIGHTS

Missing Out on Olympic Glory

After joining the U.S. Snowboard Team in 1999, Bleiler quickly proved her abilities in international competition. During the 2000 season she won an event on the World Cup circuit sponsored by the International Federation of Skiing. She also placed second in a U.S. Grand Prix event. In 2001 she claimed the U.S. National Halfpipe title and won the Vans Triple Crown of Snowboarding.

Thanks to her impressive results, Bleiler had high hopes of making the U.S. Olympic Team that would compete at the 2002 Games in Salt Lake City, Utah. But the method used to select the members of the American snowboarding squad was complicated—and controversial. Every country had the *chance* to qualify up to four snowboarders for each Olympic event. The number of athletes that actually qualified to compete for each country, though, depended upon the final standings in international World Cup competition during the 2001 season.

Bleiler and two of her teammates on the U.S. National Team, Kelly Clark and Tricia Byrnes, competed on the World Cup circuit that year and earned three spots for the United States in the Olympic women's halfpipe event at the 2002 Games. (For more information on Clark, see *Biography Today Sports*, Vol. 8.) But the three qualifiers did not automatically receive those coveted spots in the Olympics. Instead, the U.S. Ski and Snowboard Association decided to select the members of the U.S. Olympic Team based on the results of the five-event U.S. Grand Prix season in early 2002. This decision opened up the Olympic spots to a number of athletes who had chosen to compete in the two U.S. professional snowboarding tours —the U.S. Grand Prix and the Vans Triple Crown—rather than the World Cup during the 2001 season. "I feel like the people who worked for the spots are penalized, because riders who just hung out last season can go out now and get a spot,"Bleiler stated.

> **Bleiler was disappointed to miss out on her dream of competing in the 2002 Olympics."It was tough, but if I was meant to go then I would have gone," she stated."I'm bummed about it, but next time around I'll definitely be ready."**

Clark and Shannon Dunn clinched spots on the Olympic Team during the first four U.S. Grand Prix events of 2002. Bleiler performed well in these events—posting two second-place finishes—and was still in the running for the final spot on the U.S. women's halfpipe squad as the fifth and deciding event got underway in Breckenridge, Colorado. Her main competitor was her close friend Tricia Byrnes. During the competition at Breckenridge, Byrnes fell on both of her runs, while Bleiler made two strong runs and finished third overall. This left the two women tied for third place in Grand Prix points. "It was as close as it possibly could have been,"Bleiler noted.

The U.S. Ski and Snowboard Association applied three different tie-break-ing methods before finally giving the third spot on the Olympic Team to Byrnes. Upon hearing that she had narrowly defeated her friend, Byrnes burst into tears. "I was disappointed because we both deserved to go," she said. "You can't feel that good when you take something away from someone else." Bleiler was also disappointed to miss out on her dream of competing in the Olympics. "It was tough, but if I was meant to go then I would have gone," she stated. "I'm bummed about it, but next time around I'll definitely be ready." Kelly Clark went on to win the first gold medal in the halfpipe for the United States at the Salt Lake City Games.

Coming Back Strong

After watching the Olympic halfpipe competition on television, Bleiler overcame her disappointment and expressed determination to improve her own riding. "Everyone stepped it up a notch," she noted. "It was awesome to see that level of riding, and I know we can all ride like that and push the limit. It was just the Olympics that made it happen." Bleiler performed well for the remainder of the 2002 season. She won the women's halfpipe title at the U.S. Championships, claimed the Vans Triple Crown overall title, and finished second at the Sims World Championships. "I'm glad I dealt with [the disappointment] the way I did," she said afterward. "It was really hard for me that I wasn't going [to the Olympics], but I just kind of moved on and did well in all the competitions afterward."

As it turned out, however, Bleiler's strong performances at the end of 2002 only hinted at what was to come. She dominated the competition throughout the 2003 season, winning an unprecedented eight consecutive halfpipe events. Bleiler started out the season by winning a Vans Triple Crown event at Mammoth Mountain and the American Snowboard Tournament at June Mountain, both in California. These results gave her a great deal of confidence entering the Winter X Games in Aspen. "It would be awesome to podium at the X Games in front of the hometown fans," she acknowledged.

At the 2003 X Games Bleiler competed before 10,000 supportive fans. The crowd included 380 of the 470 students enrolled in her former high school, all of whom skipped class in order to watch her compete (the principal ended up giving them an excused absence). Bleiler suffered a slight case of nerves in the qualifying round and fell while attempting an inverted trick. "It was awesome to hear the crowd," she noted. "But the support can be both good and bad. There is a lot of pressure. So I had to really concentrate on the basics in my second run." She nailed the second qualifying run, moving up from last place to first place in the standings. Her impressive performance continued in the finals, where her two runs earned an amazing 95.33-point score from the judges.

Bleiler claimed her fourth straight halfpipe victory at a U.S. Grand Prix event in February 2003. Her first run of the finals was so far superior to the competition that she was virtually assured of victory. She then decided to

Bleiler does a frontside crippler over the crowd during the halfpipe finals at the 2003 U.S. Open Snowboarding Championships.

make her second run memorable for the fans by attempting a new trick, called a crippler 720. Up to this point, Bleiler's signature move was a difficult trick called a crippler 540 (a back flip with a 540-degree spin, or one-and-a-half rotations, and a blind landing). She had only attempted a crippler 720 (two full rotations) once before in competition, and on that occasion she had taken a hard fall on the top of the pipe and given herself a black eye. Nevertheless, she decided that the time was right to try it again. "The more I did the crippler 540, I was starting to overrotate it," she explained. "So it wasn't a huge step." Bleiler started her final run with a crippler 540 and finished it with a crippler 720, becoming the first woman ever to complete two cripplers in a single run. Her performance earned 48.60 points from the judges, which was the highest single-run score ever awarded to a woman in halfpipe history.

———— " ————

"It was awesome to hear the crowd," Bleiler said about the 2003 X Games. "But the support can be both good and bad. There is a lot of pressure. So I had to really concentrate on the basics in my second run."

———— " ————

Bleiler claimed her fifth straight half-pipe title two weeks later, when she dominated the Women's World Superpipe Championships in Park City, Utah. Then she racked up her sixth consecutive title at Bear Mountain in California. "I've been on an amazing roll this year," she acknowledged. "Every time you win you get this boost of confidence and you win more. It's a snowball thing." Bleiler's seventh straight win came at the U.S. Open in Mount Bachelor, Oregon. She completed her amazing string of victories at the U.S. Snowboard Grand Prix Final in Buttermilk Mountain, Colorado. "Winning seven in a row was amazing, and I honestly didn't think there was any way I could do it again," she said afterward. "But I did. I don't know how. I just put the game face on and went for it." Her unprecedented feat of eight consecutive wins helped her claim the Vans Triple Crown title and the U.S. Grand Prix championship for 2003.

Enjoying the Benefits of Success

Bleiler had been dropped by her board sponsor, Salomon, in late 2002. Throughout her remarkable 2003 season, she rode a K2 Mix snowboard. "The first time I rode the Mix in competition, I won," she recalled. "Then I went on to win seven more on that same board." After the 2003 season ended, Bleiler signed a three-year sponsorship agreement with K2. Bleiler was also selected as Female Rider of the Year in the *Transworld Snowboarding* annual riders' poll, and she was invited to appear in the 2003 film *Warren Miller's Journey*.

As 2004 approached, Bleiler looked forward to performing in an all-women snowboard video and defending her titles in the major snowboarding competitions. Unfortunately, she tore the anterior cruciate ligament in her knee in December 2003. She had surgery to repair the damage, but the injury kept her off the slopes for the entire 2004 season. Bleiler still attended many of the events, though, and provided TV commentary for the Winter X Games halfpipe competition. She also helped promote the X Games by posing nude for *FHM* and *ESPN The Magazine*. "I kept thinking, 'This isn't me at all,'" she recalled of the photo shoots. "But it's good for the Games and good for the sport, and it turned out better than I expected." Bleiler repeated as *Transworld Snowboarding's* Female Rider of the Year in 2004, and she was also nominated for the prestigious Laureus World Sport Award as Alternative Action Sports Person of the Year.

> "I'm psyched to be back, and I'm happy with my riding overall," Bleiler said after returning to competition in 2005. "But this whole contest has been really hard for me mentally. I forgot what it was like to compete. It's going to take a couple contests to get used to it again."

As she worked to recover from her injury, Bleiler decided to quit the U.S. Snowboard Team and join a group of fellow professional riders in creating an independent team called The Collection. "The reason we started our own team was the politics involved in the U.S. team," she explained. "People who don't have anything to do with snowboarding were controlling what we could and couldn't do." Bleiler and her teammates — Kelly Clark, Andy Finch, Luke Mitrani, and Ross Powers — hired their own coach, physical therapist, and manager. Their manager handles all travel arrangements, transports their gear to competitions, and provides a 32-foot luxury motor home where the athletes can relax at events. The riders have found that the team arrangement allows them to focus all their energy on snowboarding. "It just makes sense to create a team that supports you throughout the season," Bleiler stated. "I think it is the future of the sport."

Bleiler returned to competition at the beginning of the 2005 season, finishing fourth at the U.S. Snowboard Grand Prix in Breckenridge, Colorado.

Bleiler's return to competition at the U.S. Snowboard Grand Prix earned her fourth place.

"I'm psyched to be back, and I'm happy with my riding overall," she said afterward. "But this whole contest has been really hard for me mentally. I forgot what it was like to compete. It's going to take a couple contests to get used to it again." Bleiler regained her old form at the Winter X Games in late January. Competing in front of a huge hometown crowd in Aspen, she nailed a huge Crippler 720 to claim the gold medal in the women's halfpipe. "I'm just so excited. It's just unbelievable," she said of the victory. "After my knee injury, it's been hard to come back confidence-wise. But everyone supports me here so much, and tonight it just clicked."

Following her second X Games gold medal, Bleiler showed that her comeback was complete by winning the women's halfpipe competition at the Gravity Games in March. She thrilled the crowd by landing a frontside 900 (2½ rotations) in a run she later described as "the best of my career." Her dominance continued at the 2005 U.S. Open Snowboarding Championships, where she hit another frontside 900 to lock up first place. "It's fun to be back," she noted. "Last year was hard, sitting out the whole time, but watching the girls motivated me. The level of riding for women is insane right now."

Although Bleiler specializes in the halfpipe and superpipe, she hopes to improve her skills in the other snowboarding disciplines in order to avoid being pigeonholed as a "pipe jockey." "I just want to be an all-around rider

———— " ————

"Gretchen is one of the few women freestylers that angulates really well," said her former coach, Pete DelGuidice. "She can flip, get good air, and throw good spins and she does it all with style. Gretchen is pretty gutsy. We have to work to keep her in one piece because she just wants to excel so much and chasing her desire to be the best can lead to bumps and bruises."

———— " ————

and get known in the mags and films," she explained. Her former coach, Pete DelGuidice, believes that she has a future in freestyle competitions. "Gretchen is one of the few women freestylers that angulates really well. She can flip, get good air, and throw good spins and she does it all with style," he said. "Gretchen is pretty gutsy. We have to work to keep her in one piece because she just wants to excel so much and chasing her desire to be the best can lead to bumps and bruises."

Bleiler tells young fans to work hard to be the best they can be. "Put 100 percent into everything you do to reach your goals," she advised. "Always know what your goals are and go after them with the big picture in mind." Bleiler is focused on her own goal of making the U.S. Olympic Snowboard Team that will compete at the 2006 Winter Games in Turin, Italy. "I definitely want to go to the Olympics in 2006," she declared. "That is a big one for me after I missed the Salt Lake games. I also want to become a better overall rider, really solid, one of the best women's riders out there."

HOME AND FAMILY

Bleiler, who is single, lives in Snowmass Village, Colorado.

HOBBIES AND OTHER INTERESTS

In her spare time, Bleiler enjoys mountain biking, hiking, yoga, and reading. She also likes listening to music by such artists as Wu Tang, Tribe Called Quest, Nelly Furtado, and Britney Spears.

HONORS AND AWARDS

U.S. National Snowboarding Championships, Women's Halfpipe: 2001, gold medal; 2002, gold medal; 2003, gold medal; 2005, gold medal
Vans Triple Crown Series, Women's Halfpipe: 2001, first overall; 2002, first overall; 2003, first overall

U.S. Grand Prix Series, Women's Halfpipe: 2002, first overall; 2003, first
   overall
World Superpipe Championships: 2002, silver medal; 2003, gold medal
Winter X Games, Women's Halfpipe: 2003, gold medal; 2005, gold medal
Female Rider of the Year (*Transworld Snowboarding* Riders Poll): 2003, 2004
Gravity Games, Women's Halfpipe: 2005, gold medal

FURTHER READING

Periodicals

American Ski Coach, Fall 2003, p.34
Denver Post, Dec. 16, 2002, p.C1; Apr. 7, 2003, p.D3; Jan. 19, 2005, p.D9;
   Jan. 30, 1995, p.B14
Denver Rocky Mountain News, Apr. 7, 2003, p.C21; Jan. 21, 2004, p.C22;
   Jan. 24, 2004, p.B18; Mar. 9, 2005, p.C22
New York Times, Mar. 21, 2005, p.D9
Oregonian, Feb. 10, 2003, p.E1
Sports Illustrated for Kids, May 2004, p.11
Sports Illustrated Women, Dec. 2001-Jan. 2002, p.26

Online Articles

http://www.skiracing.com
   (*Ski Racing,* "Hydropower: From Water to Ice to Snow, Snowboarder
   Gretchen Bleiler Has Finally Found Her Element,"Dec. 27, 2002)
http://expn.go.com/xgames
   (EXPN.com, "Aspen's Bleiler Golden in Colorado,"Jan. 31, 2003)
http://outside.away.com
   (*Outside,* "XX Factor,"Dec. 2003)

ADDRESS

Gretchen Bleiler
The Collection, c/o Octagon
800 Connecticut Avenue
2nd Floor
Norwalk, CT 06854

WORLD WIDE WEB SITES

http://www.usoc.org
http://expn.go.com/athletes/bios

Lynne Cox 1957-

American Open-Water Endurance Swimmer
Has Endured Longer Periods of Time in Colder Water
than Anyone in History

BIRTH

Lynne Elaine Cox was born on January 2, 1957, in Boston, Massachusetts. Her father, Albert Percy Cox, was a radiologist. Her mother, Estelle Marie Cox, was an artist. She has an older brother, David, and two younger sisters, Ruth and Laura.

YOUTH

Cox grew up in New Hampshire, where her parents taught her to swim at an early age. "My parents were a stable influence of encouragement," she related. "I remember that they gave us swimming lessons in the bathtub when we were really little." From the time that she was three years old, Cox swam in the cold, clear waters of Snow Pond in Maine, where her family spent the summers at her grandfather's cabin. "I've always loved the sound, feeling, smell, look, and taste of water," she noted. "I think it has to do with growing up on the East Coast. My parents, my brother, and my sisters and I were always swimming in either sweet, open-water ponds or in the Atlantic Ocean."

"I've always loved the sound, feeling, smell, look, and taste of water," Cox noted. "I think it has to do with growing up on the East Coast. My parents, my brother, and my sisters and I were always swimming in either sweet, open-water ponds or in the Atlantic Ocean."

Cox's love of water led her to join a local swim team. One of her most memorable childhood experiences involved practicing at an outdoor pool during a storm. Nine-year-old Cox continued swimming through wind, rain, and hail, while most of her teammates retreated indoors. Instead of being afraid of the storm, she reveled in coming into such close contact with the power of nature. "That day, I realized that nature was strong, beautiful, dramatic, and wonderful, and being out in the water during that storm made me feel somehow a part of it, somehow connected to it," she remembered. "As I pulled my arms through the water, I felt as if I were swimming through a giant bowl of icy tapioca." When a teammate's mother found Cox in the pool, she was so impressed by the youngster's determination that she predicted Cox would someday swim across the English Channel (a distance of 21 miles separating France and Great Britain). This comment inspired her swimming for many years.

With the support of their parents, Cox and her siblings became strong competitive swimmers. In 1969 their parents decided to move the family to Los Alamitos, California, so the children could swim year-round and train with top coaches. Lynne ended up working with Don Gambril, a college swim coach who went on to coach the 1984 U.S. Olympic Swim Team. Although Cox was never one of the fastest swimmers in the pool, she possessed rare stamina that enabled her to maintain or even increase her speed while swimming long distances. Gambril eventually realized that there were no competitive races long enough to take advantage of Cox's unusual endurance (the longest Olympic race distance for women was only 800 meters, or about half a mile). So he suggested that she try open-water endurance racing. "I didn't really have a natural ability," Cox noted. "It was more that in doing long workouts I wouldn't quit after swimming five or six miles, and the coach realized that the last mile I did would be faster than the first."

Cox followed her coach's advice and entered the Seal Beach Rough Water Swim in 1971. In an open competition against men and women of various ages, the 14-year-old finished second in the two-mile event and third in the three-mile event. She also discovered that she loved the freedom of swimming long distances in the cool ocean, compared to the repetition of swimming laps in a heated pool. "Suddenly I felt released from a cage. I was actually going somewhere, not merely back and forth. I felt exhilarated by the challenge of swimming against the current and into the waves," she recalled. "I just really enjoy swimming on my own in wide-open waters, where a lap is one mile or as long as I want it to be."

> "Suddenly I felt released from a cage," Cox said about the freedom of swimming long distances in the cool ocean instead of swimming laps in a heated pool. "I was actually going somewhere, not merely back and forth. I felt exhilarated by the challenge of swimming against the current and into the waves. I just really enjoy swimming on my own in wide-open waters, where a lap is one mile or as long as I want it to be."

EDUCATION

Although Cox was always a good student, her shyness made it difficult for her to fit in when her family first moved from New Hampshire to California. During her years at Los Alamitos High School, however, she made friends and grew more outgoing. By the time she graduated in 1975, she had already accomplished several remarkable swimming feats and been profiled in *Sports Illustrated*. Cox continued her education at the University of California at Santa Barbara, earning a bachelor's degree in history in 1979. Her study of history gave her a strong interest in world events and contributed to her desire to complete swims that promote peace and goodwill between nations.

CAREER HIGHLIGHTS

Setting Early Records

Shortly after completing the Seal Beach Rough Water Swim in 1971, Cox joined a group of young swimmers attempting to swim across the Catalina Channel, where the Pacific Ocean flows between Catalina Island and the Los Angeles coast. Strong currents increased the straight-line distance of 21 miles to a swim of 27 miles, but Cox still managed to finish in 12 hours, 36 minutes.

In 1972, when she was a 15-year-old high school student, Cox achieved her dream of swimming across the English Channel. The channel's cold water, strong currents, and constant boat traffic make swimming across very difficult. In fact, this feat is widely considered to be the "Mount Everest" of open-water endurance swimming. Swimmers hoping to set a record are not allowed to wear wetsuits to protect themselves from the cold and must be accompanied by a qualified guide boat that tracks weather conditions and traffic.

During her first attempt to cross the channel, strong currents forced Cox to swim an S-shaped route that extended the straight-line distance of 21 miles to an actual swim of 31 miles. But she still managed to complete the crossing in 9 hours, 57 minutes, beating the previous record for men and women by 26 minutes. Her record stood for only three weeks, however, before a male swimmer beat it by 13 minutes. But Cox returned the following year and set a new record with a time of 9 hours, 36 minutes, despite swimming a total distance of 33 miles.

In 1974 Cox made a solo attempt to swim across the Catalina Channel. She was aiming for a record that had been set by her older brother, David, who was then attending college on a swimming

Cox pauses for refreshments during her English Channel swim.

scholarship. She swam at night, accompanied by a guide boat full of friends and family members, in order to take advantage of favorable currents and weather conditions. "It was such a neat night," she recalled. "The stars were out and I could even see falling stars. The moon was up, and as it went down it turned orange. The water was phosphorescent." Cox reached the shore of Catalina Island in 8 hours, 48 minutes, beating her brother's record by 2 minutes.

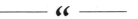

"We used to have [trophies] displayed all over the place, but I was done with that. They went into a box, and then in the trash. I don't swim for that anymore." Instead, Cox decided to use her athletic abilities to try to break down barriers between people and nations. "My goal is not just to be a great swimmer. I think people identify with the athletic struggle, and I am trying to use sports to help bring people together."

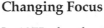

Changing Focus

In 1975, shortly after graduating from high school, Cox set out to attempt another challenging international swim. She hoped to become the first woman to swim across the Cook Strait in New Zealand. Although the distance is only 12 miles, the strait is notorious for its strong currents and large waves. In fact, only 20 people had ever attempted to swim across before Cox, and only three of those attempts had succeeded.

Like the others before her, Cox encountered difficulties during her swim. Powerful winds and waves as high as eight feet pushed her off course, so that after swimming for five hours she found herself further from the finish than she had been when she started. Cox grew discouraged and considered giving up the attempt. On board her guide boat, however, was a radio reporter who was broadcasting live updates on her progress across New Zealand. People were captivated by the story and began calling the radio station with words of encouragement for Cox. The reporter relayed some of the messages to Cox as she swam, and this raised her spirits enough to continue.

As she neared the end of her swim, Cox became exhausted and came close to quitting again. But then a large group of dolphins began swimming along with her. The dolphins jumped, danced, chattered, and whistled as they kept her company for more than an hour, helping her to complete the swim in 12 hours, 2.5 minutes. Church bells rang across New Zealand in celebration of her feat.

Cox was deeply gratified by the reception she received in New Zealand. "More than anything I now understood that no one achieves great goals alone. It didn't matter to New Zealanders that I wasn't from their country. It only mattered that I was trying to swim their strait. They had cheered me on for hours, and in doing so, they had cheered the same human spirit within themselves," she stated. "During the Cook Strait swim, we were united in a human endurance struggle that surpassed national borders."

After returning home from New Zealand, Cox began shifting her

Cox swimming alongside the Queen Mary *in California.*

focus in swimming away from setting records. In fact, she threw away the many trophies that she had won over the years. "We used to have them displayed all over the place, but I was done with that," she explained. "They went into a box, and then in the trash. I don't swim for that anymore." Instead, Cox decided to use her athletic abilities to try to break down barriers between people and nations. "My goal is not just to be a great swimmer," she acknowledged. "I think people identify with the athletic struggle, and I am trying to use sports to help bring people together."

Breaking Down Barriers

Over the next dozen years, Cox completed a series of difficult swims all over the world. In 1976 she set records for swimming to Sweden from both Norway and Denmark. She also became the first person to swim across the Strait of Magellan, which separates the southern tip of South America from the islands of Tierra del Fuego. In 1977 she became the first person to swim across three channels in the Aleutian Islands, which stretch westward from the Alaskan mainland. In 1979 Cox made one of her most dangerous swims, around the Cape of Good Hope at the southern tip of Africa. In addition to jellyfish, sea snakes, and 20-foot waves, Cox encountered a 12-foot shark that would have bitten her if a diver on her guide boat had not shot it with a spear gun. Her achievements continued in the 1980s, with successful swims in Japan, Iceland, Spain, Italy, Turkey, China, and across the United States.

Cox used all of these swims to prepare herself for a historic swim across the Bering Strait, a narrow passage that separates the United States from the Soviet Union. When Cox began planning her Bering Strait swim in the late 1970s, these two world powers were engaged in a tense struggle for political and military superiority known as the Cold War. As a result of the tensions between the two nations, Cox had to overcome numerous logistical hurdles in order to gain permission to make the swim. Her goal was to swim a distance of 2.7 miles between Little Diomede Island, off the west coast of Alaska, and Big Diomede Island (also known as Ratmanov Island), off the east coast of Siberia. She hoped that swimming from the United States to the Soviet Union would demonstrate how close the two countries were and perhaps help to bridge their differences. "There are no borders in the oceans, just imaginary lines dividing countries," Cox noted. "People might believe in those lines less if I swim across them."

> "
>
> "The sea was like a washing machine, churning up the cold water from below," Cox said about swimming in the Bering Sea. "I said to myself, 'What happens if the current sweeps me back out to sea? With the fatigue and the cold I won't be able to fight it.'"
>
> "

Cox had to endure dangerously cold water in order to swim across the Bering Strait. She tried to acclimate her body to the cold by wearing light clothing year-round, sleeping with the windows open and without covers on her bed, and gaining weight in order to increase the layer of fat insulating her vital organs. She also completed several practice swims in extremely cold water. In Alaska's Glacier Bay, for instance, she swam one mile in 38-degree water, navigating an obstacle course of ice chunks along the way.

Cox finally obtained permission from the Soviet Union to attempt her Bering Strait swim in August 1987. The water was 42 degrees when she entered it and dropped to 38 degrees during her swim. "The sea was like a washing machine, churning up the cold water from below," she remembered. "I said to myself, 'What happens if the current sweeps me back out to sea? With the fatigue and the cold I won't be able to fight it.'"

Cox swam across the Bering Strait wearing only a bathing cap and swimsuit, despite the frigid 42-degree water.

As a precaution, Cox was accompanied by a team of doctors in traditional Eskimo boats called umiaks. The doctors monitored her internal body temperature using a "radio pill"—she swallowed a small electronic thermometer that transmitted readings to a radio receiver on board one of the guide boats. These tests showed that Cox's core temperature actually increased from a normal 98.6 degrees to 100.7 degrees during the swim because of the exertion. Her body reacted to the cold by constricting the blood vessels in her skin and limbs, thus concentrating the flow of warm blood to her heart, lungs, and brain.

Cox successfully completed her crossing of the Bering Strait in 2 hours, 6 minutes. When she climbed out of the icy water and stepped onto the shore of Big Diomede Island, she was greeted by a cheering crowd of Soviets who wrapped her in towels, interviewed her for national radio and television, and then ushered her into a warming tent filled with buffet tables of food. "It was overwhelming on the snowbank," she recalled. "Microphones, people throwing towels, the realization that we'd made it—we were in the Soviet Union! But my legs were trembling and I felt I was going to fall down." As it turned out, Cox's body temperature plunged to a dangerous 94 degrees shortly after she stopped swimming. Once she emerged from the water, her blood began flowing back into her limbs, which had cooled to the temperature of the water. When this cooled blood returned to her body's core, her temperature dropped and she began shivering uncontrollably. She soon recovered, however, with the help of Soviet doctors.

Cox's swim of the Bering Strait marked the first time in nearly 50 years that anyone had been allowed to cross the U.S.-Soviet border. In fact, one of the American Eskimo guides who had accompanied her to Siberia was reunited with family members that he had not seen for decades. Cox was gratified by the impact her swim had on the people of both countries. "It was one of those rare occasions in life when things turn out better than you ever imagined," she said. "And I could see from the eyes of the Russians that it was special for them too." Three months later, the United States and Soviet Union reached an agreement that opened the Alaska-Siberia border, allowing the Eskimo families that lived in the region to interact freely. "The borders were open to them, and they were allowed to move and talk to each other, and to see what had happened to their families after so many years," Cox observed. "That makes me feel good."

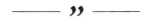

"Last summer it took one brave American by the name of Lynne Cox just two hours to swim from one of our countries to the other," said Soviet leader Mikhail Gorbachev. "We saw on television how sincere and friendly the meeting was between our people and the Americans when she stepped onto the Soviet shore. She proved by her courage how close to each other our peoples live."

In December 1987, Soviet Premier Mikhail Gorbachev traveled to Washington, D.C., to sign a historic arms control agreement that reduced the quantities of nuclear weapons held by each country. Although the agreement had been in the works for some time, Cox's historic swim provided inspiration to finalize the deal. In fact, Gorbachev acknowledged Cox at the signing ceremony. "Last summer it took one brave American by the name of Lynne Cox just two hours to swim from one of our countries to the other," the Soviet leader stated. "We saw on television how sincere and friendly the meeting was between our people and the Americans when she stepped onto the Soviet shore. She proved by her courage how close to each other our peoples live." Cox's contribution to world peace was later honored by Pope John Paul II at the Vatican and by President Ronald Reagan at the White House.

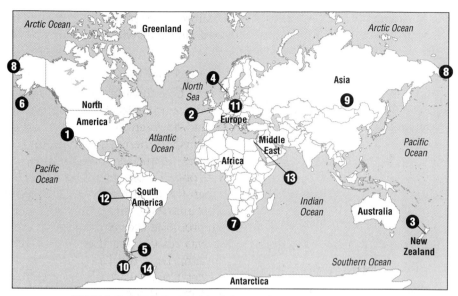

THE LOCATIONS OF SOME OF COX'S SWIMS

1. Catalina Channel
2. English Channel
3. Cook Strait
4. North Sea
5. Strait of Magellan
6. Aleutian Islands
7. Cape of Good Hope
8. Bering Strait
9. Lake Baikal
10. Beagle Channel
11. Spree River
12. Lake Titicaca
13. Gulf of Aqaba
14. Antarctica

Making History

The publicity Cox received as a result of her historic crossing of the Bering Strait led to a number of opportunities to attempt other impressive feats around the world. In 1988 she returned to the Soviet Union and swam across Lake Baikal, the world's deepest lake. She received a hero's welcome, as thousands of Russians lined the shores of the lake and threw bouquets of flowers into the water as she swam past.

In 1990 Cox traveled to South America and swam across the Beagle Channel, which separates Chile and Argentina. She convinced the governments of both countries—which were engaged in a longstanding armed dispute—to cooperate and provide escort boats for her attempt. She negotiated fierce currents to complete the seven-mile swim, which received extensive media coverage in South America. A year later, representatives of Chile and Argentina met to settle their differences.

Also in 1990, Cox swam across the Spree River to celebrate the fall of the Berlin Wall and the reuniting of East and West Germany. "The idea is to

29

swim from East Berlin to West Berlin to symbolize the opening," she explained. "I think that it shows that individuals as a group can make great changes occur. That's what happened to make the wall come down." During this swim, Cox had to endure severe water pollution and the threat of hidden mines and barbed wire in the river.

In 1992 Cox swam across Lake Titicaca on the border of Peru and Bolivia. Located at an elevation of 12,500 feet in the Andes Mountains, it is the world's highest navigable lake. The high altitude left Cox struggling to breathe, and she was bitten by an unknown waterborne organism that left welts all over her body, but she still managed to complete the crossing in 3 hours, 48 minutes. "I thought that swimming at 12,500 feet would be challenging, but I didn't expect it to be as challenging," she recalled. "Just getting used to trying to breathe at that altitude, getting used to the water, and then facing whatever was in the water."

In 1994 Cox traveled to the Middle East to swim across the Gulf of Aqaba in the Red Sea. She swam from Egypt to Israel and then from Israel to Jordan, symbolically following the path of peace agreements between those countries. "Some of my past swims have helped open borders, so I believed that a swim that traced the process of peace and celebrated it could have a similar effect," she explained. "I believe that sometimes just by seeing something small happen, something that is quite positive, other people realize that they can do something too, something larger."

Contributing to Medical Research

Over the course of her remarkable career as an open-water endurance swimmer, Cox has spent longer periods of time in colder waters than any other person in recorded history. In all of her swims, regardless of the water temperature, she wears only a swimsuit, bathing cap, and goggles. She never wears a wetsuit or applies lanolin grease for warmth, and she never uses a shark cage for protection. She not only considers such aids to be "cheating," but she also finds them impractical. "If I went into hypothermia [a condition characterized by a dangerously low body temperature] and I were covered with grease, it would be really hard to pull me out of the water," she noted. "Besides, the animal smell from the fat could attract sharks, and I don't want to be somebody's breakfast."

Cox's ability to withstand extremely cold water temperatures for hours — when most people would die within minutes of exposure — has attracted a great deal of interest from doctors and scientists. Cox has willingly served as the subject of numerous experiments to uncover the physical advantages that allow her to survive in the cold. She hopes that these experiments will help scientists gain a better understanding of how the human body regulates its temperature and recovers from exposure to very low temperatures. "I figured I could help them learn about hypothermia and survival," Cox explained.

Doctors attribute Cox's ability to withstand cold water temperatures to a combination of factors. For example, she has a high percentage of body fat (35 percent, compared to around 25 percent for an average woman) that is evenly distributed. This body fat not only provides insulation against the cold, but it also gives her body the same density as sea water, allowing her to float easily on the ocean surface. When she swims, this added buoyancy enables her to expend energy on moving forward and staying warm rather than on staying afloat. Cox's swimming style also helps her combat the cold. She relies primarily on upper body strength to pull through the water with her arms, while using her legs more like a rudder for directional control. This allows her body to shut off blood flow to her legs, retaining more warmth in her trunk. Finally, Cox has spent many years acclimating physically to the cold and training mentally to shut out its painful sensations.

—————— **"** ——————

Cox never wears a wetsuit, or applies lanolin grease for warmth, or uses a shark cage for protection. "If I went into hypothermia [a condition characterized by a dangerously low body temperature] and I were covered with grease, it would be really hard to pull me out of the water," she noted. "Besides, the animal smell from the fat could attract sharks, and I don't want to be somebody's breakfast."

—————— **"** ——————

Swimming to Antarctica

Around 2000 Cox expanded her purposes in swimming beyond challenging herself and trying to break down barriers between people. She decided to explore the limits of the human body's ability to withstand cold water temperatures. To accomplish this goal, she decided to swim in the ocean off the coast of Antarctica — the coldest place on earth. "I wanted to do something extraordinary," she stated. "The Antarctica swim was about exploring my own outer limits — exploring an area where few have ever been, and simply seeing what I could do."

Cox spent the next two years preparing for her Antarctic swim. She worked out with a trainer to increase her strength, gained 12 pounds to

Cox swam over one mile in the frigid 32-degree water off the coast of Antarctica, with no protection from the cold except for a bathing suit and bathing cap.

increase her body's insulation, grew her hair long to pile inside her bathing cap to retain heat, and underwent dental treatments to protect her teeth from cracking in the cold. In several interviews, Cox claimed that she modeled her physical preparations after the animals that lived in Antarctic waters. "If you look at the marine mammals in Antarctica, the whales, the walruses, the seals all have body fat to stay warm," she noted. "Their blubber is very dense whereas mine will be more like a cotton sweater. But I'm not going to be in as long as they are." Commentator Shelby Murphy expressed admiration for Cox's positive body image. "Not many women in this culture that abhors fat are courageous enough to compare themselves to whales," she wrote. "But that is what sets Lynne apart. She understands that even though her body doesn't conform to the rail-thin standards set by the fashion industry, she's not in her swimming suit to model it. Her purpose is higher than that."

Cox finally attempted her Antarctic swim in December 2002. She traveled to Antarctica by boat, along with a television crew from the news program "60 Minutes II." Her plan involved anchoring the support boat one mile from shore and swimming to the Antarctic continent. After scouting possible landing sites, Cox chose a rocky beach where she could climb out of the water safely. Then she waited for ideal wind, wave, and ice conditions to make her swim. Even with ideal conditions, however, Cox knew that this would be the most dangerous swim she had ever attempted. Both the air and water temperature were 32 degrees, and only one person (an Icelandic fisherman) had ever been known to survive immersion in such cold water for more than a few minutes. "I really didn't know how long I could last or if I would be okay," Cox admitted. "It was a huge leap when I jumped into that water."

Immediately after jumping in, Cox felt numbed by the cold and struggled to catch her breath. "My arms were 32 degrees, as cold as the sea," she recalled. "They were going numb, and so were my legs. I pulled my hands right under my chest so that I was swimming on the upper inches of the sea, trying to minimize my contact with the water. I was swimming fast and it was hard to get enough air. I began to notice that the cold was pressurizing my body like a giant tourniquet. It was squeezing the blood from the exterior part of my body and pushing it into the core. Everything felt tight."

Cox fought through the cold and swam as hard as she could toward shore. About halfway to her goal, she started to feel a little bit more comfortable. "Something clicked, as if my body had gained equilibrium," she remembered.

> "My arms were 32 degrees, as cold as the sea," she recalled about jumping into the Antarctic. "They were going numb, and so were my legs. I pulled my hands right under my chest so that I was swimming on the upper inches of the sea, trying to minimize my contact with the water. I was swimming fast and it was hard to get enough air. I began to notice that the cold was pressurizing my body like a giant tourniquet. It was squeezing the blood from the exterior part of my body and pushing it into the core. Everything felt tight."

"It had fully closed down the blood flow in my skin and fingers and toes. My arms and legs were as cold as the water, but I could feel the heat radiating deep within my torso and head, and this gave me confidence. I knew that my body was protecting my brain and vital organs."

As she neared the shore, Cox was delighted when a flock of penguins dove into the water and began swimming along with her. "One hundred yards from shore, I saw chinstrap penguins sliding headfirst, like tiny black toboggans, down a steep snowbank," she related. "They waddled across the beach at full tilt, holding their wings out at their sides for balance. Reaching the water, they dove in headfirst, then porpoised across it, clearing it by one or two feet with each surface dive. . . . They zoomed under me in bursts of speed, and their bubbles exploded like white fireworks. More penguins joined in. One cannonballed off a ledge, another slipped on some ice and belly flopped, and three penguins swam within inches of my hands. I reached out to touch one, but he swerved and flapped his wings, so he moved just beyond my fingertips. I had no idea why they were swimming with me, but I knew it was a good sign; it meant there were no killer whales or leopard seals in the area."

When Cox finally reached the shore, she had completed a 1.06-mile, 25-minute swim in 32-degree water. She thus became the first person ever to swim a mile in the Antarctic, and also the first human ever known to swim with penguins in the wild. Her support team bundled her in warm towels, helped her into an inflatable boat, and rushed her back to the ship. She shivered uncontrollably while her body gradually warmed itself, but after an hour her core temperature had returned to normal. "The swim to Antarctica was the culmination of 30 years of swimming and two years of complete focus on one big goal," she said afterward. "Achieving it was satisfying, and I know that success will now allow me to do something more. It may be in swimming or another adventure—I don't know yet."

> **"**
>
> *"The swim to Antarctica was the culmination of 30 years of swimming and two years of complete focus on one big goal," Cox said afterward. "Achieving it was satisfying, and I know that success will now allow me to do something more. It may be in swimming or another adventure— I don't know yet."*
>
> **"**

Pushing the Limits

Throughout her remarkable career, Cox has earned a reputation as one of the greatest open-water endurance swimmers in history. In recognition of her many achievements, she was inducted into the International Swimming Hall of Fame in 2000. Yet she has never made much money from her swimming exploits. In fact, she has often struggled to raise the money needed to finance her international swims. Over the years, she has supported herself by working as a librarian and physical therapist, teaching swimming lessons, writing magazine articles, and giving motivational speeches. In 2004 she published a memoir about her life and swimming feats called *Swimming to Antarctica*. A reviewer for *Publishers Weekly* called it "a thrilling, awesome, and well-written story."

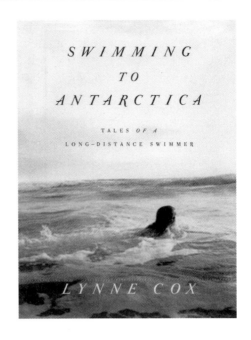

Cox continues to participate in scientific research studies to determine how her body adapts to extremely cold water. "I think it's training; I think it's genetics; I think it's the advantage of being a woman," she explained. "My body is perfect for ocean swimming—what my body does is maintain fat and layer it on. The other thing is that I have muscle mass to generate heat." While some people believe that she must be impervious to the cold, Cox claims that it does affect her. "I feel the cold just like anyone else," she stated. "When I'm training off the California coast and just getting into the water I will go in gradually. I'm lifting up my arms and doing little squeals. It's not that I don't feel the cold, it's that I just don't *focus* on it."

When asked why she attempts new and more difficult swims, Cox replies that she is largely driven by curiosity. "I want to see what is over there," she noted. "I want to see what is under that rock. I want to ask the question that I'm not supposed to ask. They say curiosity killed the cat, but they were wrong." Another important goal for Cox involves pushing the limits of the human body. "Initially it was just the athletic achievements, then athletics combined with cold research, and then it became the goodwill of trying to open borders that had been closed," she explained. "My catchphrase now is 'beyond borders'—beyond the physical limits, beyond the 'why you can't.'"

HOME AND FAMILY

Cox, who is single, lives in Los Alamitos, California.

Cox taking her first scuba dive off Catalina Island; more than 20 years earlier, at age 14, she swam across Catalina Channel.

HOBBIES AND OTHER INTERESTS

Hoping to expand upon her experiences in the water, Cox recently took up scuba diving. "It's much different than swimming," she noted. "My brain had a difficult time wrapping around it. It's been very challenging."

WRITINGS

Swimming to Antarctica: Tales of a Long-Distance Swimmer, 2004

HONORS AND AWARDS

Woman of the Year (*Los Angeles Times*): 1975
International Swimming Hall of Fame: 2000
Woman of the Year (*Glamour*): 2003

FURTHER READING

Books

Cox, Lynne. *Swimming to Antarctica: Tales of a Long-Distance Swimmer,* 2004
Great Women in Sports, 1996

Periodicals

Biography, Dec. 2003
Current Biography Yearbook, 2004
Current Science, Aug. 29, 2003, p.10
Los Angeles Times, July 12, 1985, Sports, p.14; July 12, 1987, Sports, p.16;
    Aug. 8, 1987, Metro, p.1; Sep. 1, 1988, Metro, p.3; Jan. 22, 1990, p.C13;
    July 1, 1992, p.C6; Oct. 16, 1994, p.E1
Los Angeles Times Magazine, Dec. 14, 1986, p.6; Sep. 6, 1987, p.20
New Yorker, Aug. 23-30, 1999, p.160; Feb. 3, 2003, p.66
Orange County (CA) Register, Aug. 28, 1987, p.B1; Jan. 31, 1988, p.J6; June 8,
    1990, p.B2
People, May 4, 1987, p.46; Aug. 24, 1987, p.32; Jan. 12, 2003, p.102
Sports Illustrated, Feb. 3, 1975, p.54; Feb. 17, 1975, p.16; Feb. 17, 2003, p.11
Women's Sports and Fitness, Apr. 1993, p.36

Online Articles

http://www.cbsnews.com
    (*CBSNews.com,* "Swimming to Antarctica," Sep. 17, 2003)
http://www.newyorker.com
    (*New Yorker Online,* "Swimming with the Penguins," Feb. 3, 2003)
http://www.womenof.com
    (*Womenof.com,* "A Body Designed on Purpose," Feb. 24, 2003)

Online Databases

Biography Resource Center Online, 2005, article from *Great Women in Sports,*
1996

ADDRESS

Lynne Cox
Knopf Publishing/Author Mail
1745 Broadway
New York, NY 10019

WORLD WIDE WEB SITE

http://www.ishof.org

Daunte Culpepper 1977-
American Football Player with the Minnesota Vikings
Three-Time Pro Bowl Quarterback

BIRTH

Daunte (pronounced DAWN-tay) Richard Culpepper was
born on January 28, 1977, in Miami, Florida. His biological
mother, Barbara Henderson, was a teenager serving a prison
sentence for armed robbery when she gave birth to him.
Henderson managed to convince Emma Culpepper, who
worked at the prison, to adopt her infant son. Emma Culpepper was 62 years old and had already raised 14 children —
four belonging to her deceased brother, seven belonging to

her sister-in-law, and three foster children. She initially turned down the request to raise another child, but she eventually reconsidered and agreed to help the teenaged mother. Years later, Daunte established a good relationship with Henderson and her five other children, who are his younger half-brothers and sisters. He has never met his biological father.

YOUTH

Daunte grew up in Emma Culpepper's tiny house in Ocala, Florida. Although his adoptive mother expected him to follow the rules and do his chores, he always considered himself lucky to be in her care. "She was an angel to me," he stated. "She had done her part in life already. A lot of kids in my situation have fallen into a bad situation. I fell into a very, very good one. She instilled in me some of the things she believes in, like loyalty, honesty, and trust. She is the person who made me the person I am today."

When Daunte was about five years old, his biological mother was released from prison and asked Emma if she could have her son back. Emma reluctantly let Daunte go, figuring that children should be with their biological parents whenever possible. But Daunte was so upset about the change in his living situation that Barbara Henderson returned him after a couple of weeks. "I was miserable," he recalled. "I didn't know her. I knew she was my mom, but I didn't want to live with anybody but Emma. [My mother] loved me that much to take me back to Emma. She saw how unhappy I was."

> "She was an angel to me," Culpepper said about his adoptive mother, Emma Culpepper. "She had done her part in life already. A lot of kids in my situation have fallen into a bad situation. I fell into a very, very good one. She instilled in me some of the things she believes in, like loyalty, honesty, and trust. She is the person who made me the person I am today."

Daunte was an active, athletic boy who enjoyed playing basketball and baseball in his youth. He started playing football at the age of 12, and it did not take long for his coaches to recognize his extraordinary skills. "My first position was wide receiver," he remembered. "Actually, I started playing quarterback by mistake. A dude threw an incomplete pass to me and I picked up the ball and threw it back to the quarterback. My coach saw me throw. After that, he put me at quarterback. From that day on, I've been playing quarterback. That's a true story!"

EDUCATION

Culpepper attended Vanguard High School in Ocala. He was an outstanding athlete, earning varsity letters in football, basketball, baseball, and weightlifting. On the basketball court, he averaged more than 19 points and 11 rebounds per game. On the baseball field, his power at the plate convinced the New York Yankees to draft him. But it was on the football field that he truly made his mark. As a three-year starter at quarterback, Culpepper racked up more than 9,000 total yards of offense and 83 touchdowns. During his senior season alone, he passed for 3,074 yards and 31 touchdowns, while rushing for another 602 yards. He led his team all the way to the Florida state championship game, where he and his teammates lost a heartbreaker on a missed field goal as time expired. Culpepper received a number of awards for his performance, including All-American honors and Florida's Mr. Football award.

> "My first position was wide receiver," Culpepper remembered. "Actually, I started playing quarterback by mistake. A dude threw an incomplete pass to me and I picked up the ball and threw it back to the quarterback. My coach saw me throw. After that, he put me at quarterback. From that day on, I've been playing quarterback. That's a true story!"

Despite all his prowess on the gridiron, Culpepper nearly missed out on the chance to play college football. He was a very poor student for the first three years of his high school career, barely managing to pass with a 1.5 grade point average. Although he was intelligent, he did not bother to do his schoolwork. College recruiters who had been attracted by his skills as a quarterback lost interest when they saw his poor academic record. "I was always able to do the work, but I was a big procrastinator," Culpepper explained. "I always thought, 'I'll get by. I'll do something to get by.' I was at a point where I wasn't getting it done. It was a big checkpoint for me in my life."

The only college that continued to show interest in Culpepper after learning about his low grades was the University of Central Florida (UCF), located in nearby Orlando. UCF was then competing in the NCAA's second tier of college football, Division IAA, but preparing to move up to the top level, Division IA. The coaching staff was looking for a star athlete who had the potential to make it to the NFL. They knew that an athlete of that caliber could bring national attention and respect to the UCF football program.

The UCF offensive coordinator, a former high school teacher, met with Culpepper and helped him develop a plan to improve his grades so that he could become academically eligible for a college football scholarship. As part of this plan, Culpepper had to retake several classes he had failed earlier. This entailed sitting in classrooms alongside freshmen and sophomores. "Some people say it would have been humiliating because you're a senior and everybody knows who you are," Culpepper acknowledged. "I had to suck it up, swallow my pride, and go ahead and do it. I heard a lot of stuff— 'he's dumb,' 'he's stupid,' 'he can't do it.' But I went to class every day and got it done. There was no doubt in my mind I would."

Throughout his senior year, Culpepper spent every spare moment studying. He also started participating in class and seeking out teachers when he needed help. As a result of his effort, his grades improved dramatically. He earned all As and Bs his senior year, making the honor roll and raising his overall grade point average to the 2.0 he needed for a football scholarship. As soon as it appeared that Culpepper would become academically eligible, a number of big-time college football programs began recruiting him heavily. But Culpepper felt a sense of loyalty to UCF and signed a letter of intent to play football in Orlando. "UCF stayed with me all the way, so I felt I should stay with them," he explained. "Other schools backed off me. They didn't."

College — The University of Central Florida Golden Knights

After graduating from high school in 1995, Culpepper entered UCF as a freshman that fall. He immediately took over the starting quarterback job for the Golden Knights football team. In the first game of his college career, UCF played Eastern Kentucky, the fifth-ranked team in Division IAA. When Culpepper was sacked on the first snap, many fans worried that the young signal-caller would be intimidated. Instead, he came back strong to complete his next 12 passes and lead the Golden Knights to an impressive 40-32 victory. Culpepper was a bright spot for UCF the remainder of his freshman season, throwing for 2,071 yards. "My first year was everything I could have imagined," he said afterward. Unfortunately, a weak defense held the team to a 6-5 record.

During Culpepper's sophomore year in 1996 UCF moved up to the top level of college football. The Golden Knights were not expected to do well against the tougher competition in Division IA. But in the season opener they surprised many observers by making a dramatic fourth-quarter

Culpepper in action with the University of Central Florida Golden Knights against Nebraska in 1997.

comeback to defeat the College of William and Mary by a score of 39-33. UCF went on to post a respectable 5-6 record that year. Culpepper passed for 2,565 yards and 19 touchdowns during the campaign, despite being hampered by injuries, including a separated shoulder and sprained ankle.

In 1997 UCF started out the season by playing three tough opponents: the University of Mississippi, the University of South Carolina, and the University of Nebraska. Most people expected the Golden Knights to get crushed in these contests, but Culpepper and his teammates forced all three opponents to sweat out tough victories. When UCF faced Nebraska, for example, the Cornhuskers were ranked sixth in the nation and were favored to win by 42 points. But Culpepper picked apart the Nebraska defense and led his team to a surprising 17-14 halftime lead. The Cornhuskers' superior size and strength took its toll in the second half, and UCF lost the game 38-24. Still, Culpepper gained national attention for his performance. As Nebraska Coach Tom Osborne said afterward, "If he were at a more prestigious institution, you'd probably hear more about him for the Heisman," referring to the prestigious annual trophy honoring the best player in college football.

Culpepper put up amazing numbers during his junior season. He finished fourth in the nation with an average of 320 yards of total offense (passing, rushing, and receiving yards) per game. He also set 15 school records for offensive performance, including most passing yards (with 3,086) and total yards (with 3,524) in a season. He became a finalist for the Davey O'Brien Award, presented annually to the top quarterback in college football.

—— *"* ——

"I never had any second thoughts about returning to UCF for my fourth year," Culpepper explained. "My mom always taught me about loyalty. UCF stood by me. They helped me when I needed it, and now I feel the program's at a point where maybe I can help them."

—— *"* ——

Considering all the accolades he received during his junior season, many people assumed that Culpepper would opt to skip his senior year of college and make himself available for the NFL draft. But he decided to stay in school in hopes of leading UCF to its first Division IA bowl game. "I never had any second thoughts about returning to UCF for my fourth year," he explained. "My mom always taught me about loyalty. UCF stood by me. They helped me when I needed it, and now I feel the program's at a point where maybe I can help them."

Culpepper achieved great statistics once again in 1998. He passed for 3,690 yards and 28 touchdowns, and his completion rate of 73.6 percent set a new NCAA single-season record. He also rushed for 463 yards and 12 touchdowns. Culpepper thus became only the third player in NCAA history to pass for over 10,000 yards and rush for over 1,000 yards in his career. Thanks to his outstanding performance, the Golden Knights posted a 9-2 record on the season. Although that made UCF eligible for a postseason bowl game, the team was disappointed not to receive an invitation. Culpepper did receive a number of individual honors, including the Sammy Baugh National Passer of the Year Award and first-team All-American honors. He also finished sixth in voting for the Heisman Trophy.

A secondary education major, Culpepper continued applying his good study habits and maintained a solid B average at UCF. By the time he graduated in 1999, he was widely considered to be one of the top players available in the NFL draft. UCF Head Coach Mike Kruczek argued that Culpepper possessed the best physical skills of any college quarterback in the nation. "He's at the top of the list, as far as I'm concerned," he stated. "He also has a tremendous work ethic and plays the game fearlessly. With those kinds of qualities, he's going to be tough to beat."

———— " ————

"I loved everything about him," Minnesota Vikings Coach Denny Green said about watching Culpepper play during his senior year at UCF. "I loved his poise. I loved the fact that he's a classic drop-back passer, even though he can run. I loved how competitive he was and how he's got that spark, how he makes things happen. As I watched that game, it came to me that Daunte represents the new generation. Quarterbacks keep getting bigger and more athletic, and he is leading the way."

———— " ————

CAREER HIGHLIGHTS

NFL — The Minnesota Vikings

Culpepper was selected by the Minnesota Vikings with the 11th overall pick in the first round of the 1999 NFL draft. He was the fourth quarterback taken, following Tim Couch, Donovan McNabb, and Akili Smith. Some Minnesota fans criticized the team's decision to draft Culpepper. They recognized that he was a gifted young player, but they worried that he might have trouble adjusting to the professional game. They also felt that the Vikings should have used the pick to address a current need, since they already had two veteran quarterbacks in Randall Cunningham and Jeff George.

But the Vikings coaches believed that Culpepper could be the key to the team's future. At 6 feet, 4 inches tall and a solid 260 pounds, Culpepper was the biggest professional quarterback in history. He also possessed a rocket arm capable of throwing the ball 80 yards, the speed to run the 40-

yard dash in 4.6 seconds, and the agility to jump 36 inches in the air. Head Coach Denny Green remembered watching Culpepper play during his senior year at UCF: "I loved everything about him. I loved his poise. I loved the fact that he's a classic drop-back passer, even though he can run. I loved how competitive he was and how he's got that spark, how he makes things happen. As I watched that game, it came to me that Daunte represents the new generation. Quarterbacks keep getting bigger and more athletic, and he is leading the way."

For his part, Culpepper was thrilled to be selected by the Vikings, which had posted a 15-1 record the previous year. He looked forward to learning from the veteran quarterbacks and throwing to star receivers like Cris Carter, Jake Reed, and Randy Moss. "I think going to the Vikings is a great situation for me to fall into, and I feel truly blessed," he stated. Culpepper maintained his positive outlook throughout

Culpepper enjoys a moment of pride, showing off his new jersey after being selected by the Minnesota Vikings in the 1999 NFL draft.

Minnesota's roller-coaster 1999 season—when the Vikings posted a 10-6 record—despite the fact that he only appeared in one game. "I knew my rookie season would be a learning year," he noted. "I put everything into learning from players like Randall, Jeff, Cris Carter, and Randy Moss. I knew my chance would come."

Taking on the Starting Job

To the amazement of Vikings fans and many others around the league, Coach Green let both Cunningham and George go at the end of the 1999 season rather than sign them to large contracts. With both veteran quarterbacks off the team, Green announced that Culpepper would be Minnesota's new starting quarterback. "All we know is that this is a guy who's been a great performer throughout his career," the coach explained. "We're excited for him to play. We know what he can do." Many people criticized the move, noting that Culpepper had only played in one NFL game and never even thrown a pass. But Culpepper claimed that he was up for the challenge. "People haven't seen me play up here," he said. "That's why there are so many doubters. But I know my skill level. I know I'm ready to compete at this level."

Over the course of that summer, Culpepper spent two months doing drills with his two top receivers, Cris Carter and Randy Moss. He soon impressed the Viking stars with his skills, work ethic, and leadership. "The main thing I needed to do was to gain the team's respect," he acknowledged. "They are two of the main guys who are real important to my success, and I'm going to be important to their success this year. So there was no way I could have gone through this offseason without being around those guys. Not just football, but personally, getting a chance to hang out with them."

> "The main thing I needed to do was to gain the team's respect," Culpepper acknowledged. "[Cris Carter and Randy Moss] are two of the main guys who are real important to my success, and I'm going to be important to their success this year. So there was no way I could have gone through this offseason without being around those guys. Not just football, but personally, getting a chance to hang out with them."

Culpepper's hard work seemed to pay off during the 2000 season. Although he seemed a bit nervous in the season opener, he still led the Vikings to a 30-27 victory over the Chicago Bears. As the young quarterback settled in, the Vikings went on a roll, winning the next 6 games and finishing the season with a strong 11-5 record. Culpepper played in all 16 games and had a great year, completing 62.7 percent of his passes for a total of 3,937 yards and 33 touchdowns, and rushing for another 470 yards and 7 touchdowns. He progressed from appearing in one NFL game in 1999 to being named a starter in the Pro Bowl in 2000. Yet Culpepper gave the credit for his success to his offensive line. "With all those guys around me, I could sit back and just pick who I wanted to throw to," he noted. "I don't think people understood how much the other guys did."

Culpepper manages to get off a pass in this game against the New York Giants.

In the first round of the playoffs, Culpepper turned in a great performance to lead his team to a 34-16 victory over the New Orleans Saints. Afterward, he was named the NFL's Offensive Player of the Week. In the NFC championship game, however, Culpepper threw three interceptions and the Vikings were crushed by the New York Giants, 41-0. Although he was disappointed to fall one game short of playing in the Super Bowl, he expressed confidence in himself and his teammates. "There is no way I'm going to doubt myself at all," he stated. "Never, ever. Because I know what I can do. I'm not being cocky. I'm just confident in myself and the team, that we're going to get the job done."

Falling on Tough Times

As the 2001 season approached, the Vikings faced a series of challenges. The team's star running back, Robert Smith, unexpectedly announced his retirement. The offensive line suffered two significant losses, as Todd Steussie left the team as a free agent and Korey Stringer died of heat stroke in training camp. Once the season got underway, Culpepper struggled behind a makeshift line and missed five games due to a knee injury. He still passed for 2,612 yards and 14 touchdowns, and rushed for an additional 416 yards and 5 touchdowns. But the Vikings posted a disappointing 5-11 record for the season and failed to make the playoffs.

———— **❝** ————

"I made too many mistakes last year, and I wasn't mature enough to let them go," Culpepper admitted. "Now, I'll make a more conscious effort to make smart plays that keep us in games. Bad things will happen, but I have to stay on an even keel."

———— **❞** ————

Culpepper and his team continued to struggle in the 2002 season, losing five of the first six games on their way to a 6-10 record. The situation reached a low point for Culpepper during a home game against the New York Giants in November. When he made a series of bad decisions that resulted in turnovers, he was booed mercilessly by the Minnesota crowd. "I'd never heard anyone boo me," he recalled. "It woke me up, made me realize things can change like that." The new Vikings coach, Mike Tice, pulled Culpepper out of the game and sat him on the bench for the first time in his career.

Over the course of the 2002 season, Culpepper passed for 3,853 yards and 18 touchdowns, and rushed for 609 yards and 10 touchdowns. But his quarterback rating dipped to a mediocre 75.3, as he also threw a league-high 23 interceptions and fumbled 23 times. Some analysts attributed his struggles to the fact that opposing defenses adjusted their strategies to contain him. They also claimed that he often had trouble finding secondary receivers when his first option was covered.

But others blamed Culpepper's poor performance on the "Randy Ratio," the media's nickname for an unofficial offensive scheme developed by Coach Tice. In order to keep temperamental receiver Randy Moss happy and involved in the game, Tice decided that Moss should be the target of at least 40 percent of Culpepper's passes. This expectation affected Culpepper's decision-making and led him to throw passes into double and triple coverage just to get the ball to Moss. As a result, half of his interceptions that year came on passes to Moss. "It's definitely tough for me right now," Culpepper acknowledged. "I'm very accustomed to winning throughout every part of my development. But I don't feel there's anything I have to change. I've just got to play better, and everybody has to play better all the way around. When we do that, that's when we're going to start winning."

Vikings management seemed to believe that this was true. During the off-season they signed Culpepper to a 10-year contract worth $102 million, including a $16 million signing bonus, making him one of the highest-paid players in the NFL. "We put ourselves behind him and showed him that all the things we've been saying to him privately we meant, which is, 'You're the guy. If we're going to win a Super Bowl, you're the guy,'" said Coach Tice. "He's much more relaxed, it seems."

Returning to the Pro Bowl

The Vikings upgraded their offensive line for the 2003 campaign and assigned a single coach to communicate with Culpepper so that he would not be confused by mixed messages. Culpepper responded by turning in a strong year. He completed 65 percent of his passes for 3,479 yards and 25 touchdowns with only 11 interceptions, earning a solid quarterback rating of 96.4. He also rushed for 422 yards and 4 touchdowns and made the second Pro Bowl appearance of his career. "I made too many mistakes last year, and I wasn't mature enough to let them go," he admitted. "Now, I'll make a more conscious effort to make smart plays that keep us in games. Bad things will happen, but I have to stay on an even keel." The Vikings started off strong, winning the first six games of the season, but then faltered toward the end of the year. They finished the year with a 9-7 record and narrowly missed making the playoffs.

Culpepper had another great year in 2004. He completed 69.9 percent of his passes for 4,133 yards and 34 touchdowns, while throwing only 11 interceptions. His stellar performance resulted in an outstanding 110.4 quarterback rating for the season. On the ground, meanwhile, he added 361 yards rushing for 2 more touchdowns. Culpepper attributed his improvement to having greater faith in his teammates. "I've learned I don't have to be Superman," he explained. "I don't have to break tackles and throw a 50-yard bomb on every play. Sometimes you have to throw it away and let the punter do his job. I realize the big picture, that sometimes you gotta play the field-position game. I never thought about the field-position game earlier in my career." The Vikings finished 8-8 and made it to the NFC divisional

"I've learned I don't have to be Superman," Culpepper explained. "I don't have to break tackles and throw a 50-yard bomb on every play. Sometimes you have to throw it away and let the punter do his job. I realize the big picture, that sometimes you gotta play the field-position game. I never thought about the field-position game earlier in my career."

Culpepper's strong season in 2004 led the Vikings to the NFC divisional playoffs, where they lost to the Philadelphia Eagles, 27-14.

playoffs, but they were eliminated by the Philadelphia Eagles in the first round.

With his physical skills and leadership ability, many NFL insiders expect Culpepper to remain one of the top quarterbacks in the game for many years to come. "Daunte is a very vibrant person in the locker room. He's always upbeat, no matter what's going on out there," said Vikings tight end Jermaine Wiggins. "He's the type of player who's always having a good time, always has a smile on his face. And as a player, when you see your leader doing that, it makes you say everything's going to be all right."

MARRIAGE AND FAMILY

In 2002, Culpepper married Kimberly Rhem, whom he met during his senior year of high school. They have two daughters together, Lyric and Asia, and are also raising Rhem's daughter from a previous relationship, Briana. "It's absolutely wonderful that, at such a young age, I can have a family and I can go home and have that stability," Culpepper said. "I think that's awesome. It's calmed me down, and it makes me think before I react to anything. And it also gives me the fuel to work even harder. I gotta take care of them."

"She's a very, very special lady. Remarkable. Strong. Everything you'd want in a mother, in a parent," Culpepper said about his adoptive mother. "Her love was just always there. I can never repay her for what she's done for me. There's no dollar amount that I could ever give her that would amount to half of what she's done. She gave me those things that money can't buy. But I can try. I'm going to take care of her the best way I can."

Culpepper remains very close to his adoptive mother, Emma Culpepper. "She's a very, very special lady. Remarkable. Strong. Everything you'd want in a mother, in a parent," he stated. "Her love was just always there. I can never repay her for what she's done for me. There's no dollar amount that I could ever give her that would amount to half of what she's done. She gave me those things that money can't buy. But I can try. I'm going to take care of her the best way I can." For Mother's Day of 2001 he presented her with a new, fully furnished five-bedroom house with a backyard pool in a gated community near Ocala.

Culpepper also stays in touch with his biological mother, Barbara Henderson, and helps her family financially. "She's a lady who has changed her ways," he explained. "When she was young and out on the streets, she did some things that some people do. I'm just glad that she had enough in her heart to give me up."

HOBBIES AND OTHER INTERESTS

In his spare time, Culpepper enjoys relaxing by playing football video games. He is also a celebrity spokesperson for the African American Adoption Agency in St. Paul, Minnesota, which is committed to finding permanent homes for foster children of color. He has pledged over $500,000 to support the agency's work, and he often gives speeches to help dispel misconceptions people might have about adopting African-American boys.

HONORS AND AWARDS

High School Football All-American: 1994
Mr. Football (Florida Athletic Coaches Association): 1994
NCAA Football All-American: 1997, 1998
Male Amateur Athlete of the Year (Florida Sports Hall of Fame): 1997
Independent Player of the Year (*Football News*): 1998
National Offensive Player of the Year: 1998
Sammy Baugh National Passer of the Year: 1998
NFL Quarterback of the Year (National Quarterback Club): 2000
ESPY Award as Breakthrough Athlete of the Year: 2000
NFL Pro Bowl: 2000, 2003, 2004

FURTHER READING

Books

Bernstein, Ross. *Sports Great Daunte Culpepper,* 2003
Contemporary Black Biography, Vol. 32, 2002
Stewart, Mark. *Daunte Culpepper: Command and Control,* 2002
Who's Who among African Americans, 2004
Who's Who in America, 2005

Periodicals

Los Angeles Times, Aug. 16, 1998, p.C5; Aug. 25, 1998, p.C1
Miami Herald, Apr. 18, 1999, p.C14
Minneapolis Star Tribune, Oct. 27, 2002, p.V1

New York Times, Sep. 20, 1995, p.B13; Nov. 11, 2002, p.D4

St. Paul (MN) Pioneer Press, July 23, 2000, p.C4

Sport, Sep. 1998, p.66

Sports Illustrated, Sep. 11, 2000, p.64; Dec. 4, 2000, p.40; Sep. 15, 2003, p.53; Nov. 1, 2004, p.60

Sports Illustrated for Kids, Dec. 2001, p.33; Jan. 2005, p.22

Sporting News, Aug. 19, 1996, p.10; May 4, 1998, p.59; Sep. 21, 1998, p.52; Oct. 9, 2000, p.31

Time, Dec. 11, 2000, p.98

USA Today, Oct. 24, 2004, p.C1

Online Databases

Biography Resource Center Online, 2005, articles from *Contemporary Black Biography,* 2002, and *Who's Who among African Americans,* 2004

ADDRESS

Daunte Culpepper
Minnesota Vikings
9520 Viking Drive
Eden Prairie, MN 55344

WORLD WIDE WEB SITES

http://daunteculpepper.com
http://www.nfl.com
http://www.nflplayers.com
http://www.vikings.com

Julie Foudy 1971-

American Soccer Player (Retired) with the U.S.
Women's National Team
Winner of Two Olympic Gold Medals and Two
Women's World Cup Championships

BIRTH

Julie Foudy (pronounced FOW-dee) was born on January 23,
1971, in San Diego, California. She was the youngest of four
children born to Jim Foudy, a sales representative, and Judy
Foudy, a nurse. She has two older brothers, Michael and Jeffrey,
and one older sister, Kristin.

YOUTH

Foudy grew up in Mission Viejo, a quiet suburb of Los Angeles. She was an athletic girl who loved sports and always tried to keep up with her older brothers and sister. She worried her parents on many occasions by skateboarding down the hill in front of their house or jumping off the roof of their wooden patio into the backyard swimming pool. "She was very active and coordinated," her mother recalled. "And when she got hurt she didn't cry much. We have videos of her getting hit in the face with a ball, crying for just a moment, and then joining the game again. Somehow she never had to go to the emergency room."

Julie was a tomboy who played basketball and football with neighborhood boys, surfed with her brothers in the Pacific Ocean, pitched for a Little League baseball team, and refused to wear a dress throughout her childhood. "I wanted to be a boy. I acted like a boy," she admitted. "My brothers' friends used to call me 'Jimmy.'" She was also a confident, outgoing, boisterous girl who could always be counted on to tell a joke. "Growing up, I used to tell about 1,000 jokes in a row—to anyone who would listen," she remembered. "My family would pull me in and say, 'Julie, tell jokes.' So I would tell jokes for an hour."

> **"**
>
> *"She was very active and coordinated," Foudy's mother recalled. "And when she got hurt she didn't cry much. We have videos of her getting hit in the face with a ball, crying for just a moment, and then joining the game again. Somehow she never had to go to the emergency room."*
>
> **"**

Of all the activities that Julie participated in, soccer was always her favorite. By the time she reached the first grade, she was so good at dribbling the ball with her feet that older boys invited her to join in their games. She started playing on a girls' soccer team in the second grade and made the league's all-star team in her first season. She soon joined a traveling soccer team called the Soccerettes and spent the next 10 years playing in tournaments throughout California and the Southwest.

Julie loved soccer despite the fact that she had few role models in the sport. While she was growing up, the United States did not yet have a Women's National Soccer Team, and no professional soccer leagues existed for women. But she was part of the first generation of American girls to benefit from Title IX, a historic law passed in 1971 that forbids sex discrimination in federally funded education programs. Under Title IX, schools that receive money from taxpayers are required to provide equal opportunities for male and female students to participate in sports. Title IX thus had the effect of increasing the athletic opportunities open to girls and women at every level across the country.

> *Foudy was accepted to medical school, but she deferred her admission twice and finally decided to forego medical school in order to pursue soccer and other goals. "I love medicine and science," she noted, "but I wasn't sure I could devote myself to being a doctor for the next 40 years. There are too many things I want to do."*

EDUCATION

Foudy attended Del Cerro Elementary School and Mission Viejo High School. She was always an excellent student, boasting a perfect 4.0 grade point average in high school. "She was so disciplined," her mother recalled. "We never had to tell her to study. She just seemed to understand the value of an education."

Foudy was also an outstanding athlete in soccer, volleyball, and track. She made the Mission Viejo varsity girls' soccer team as a freshman in 1985. She played the midfielder position in order to take advantage of her well-rounded game and on-field leadership skills. Midfielders have been compared to quarterbacks, in that they direct the movement of their teammates and the ball. They form the first line of defense when opposing teams attack, and they are also responsible for directing their own team's offensive attack. Although midfielders do not tend to score as many goals as forwards, they nonetheless play a vital role on the soccer field.

Foudy had a huge impact on her high school team, at one point leading Mission Viejo to 84 consecutive victories. She was named Southern California Player of the Year three times, and she was honored as a high school all-American as a junior and senior. In 1989 the *Los Angeles Times* named her "Soccer Player of the Decade." The popular student was also elected homecoming queen by her classmates during her senior year. When Foudy graduated from high school in 1989, however, she was forced to miss the ceremony. By this time, she was playing with the U.S. National Women's Soccer Team.

College — The Stanford University Cardinal

Thanks to her skills on the soccer field, Foudy was recruited by dozens of colleges. But she ultimately decided to attend Stanford University because of its strong academic reputation. Since Stanford did not offer athletic scholarships for women's soccer at that time, Foudy paid for her college education through grants, loans, and help from her parents.

Foudy became a superstar for Stanford's soccer team. As a freshman, she was voted her team's most valuable player as well as the NCAA Freshman of the Year. She was named a first-team collegiate all-American three times, selected as a junior as Player of the Year by *Soccer America*, and led the Cardinal to the NCAA tournament all four years. She finished her college career as Stanford's all-time leader in goals (with 52) and assists (with 36).

Playing soccer for the Stanford Cardinal.

Foudy also continued to excel in the classroom during her years at Stanford, earning a bachelor's degree in human biology in 1993. After graduating, she received top scores on her medical school entrance exams and was accepted to Stanford's prestigious medical program in 1994. Foudy deferred her admission twice — once to play in the 1995 Women's World Cup and again to play in the 1996 Olympic Games — and finally decided to forego medical school in order to pursue soccer and other goals. "I love medicine and science," she noted, "but I wasn't sure I could devote myself to being a doctor for the next 40 years. There are too many things I want to do."

CAREER HIGHLIGHTS

Foudy is part of the first generation of superstars in women's soccer. Nicknamed "Loudy Foudy" by her teammates, she was a co-captain and midfielder for the legendary U.S. Women's National Soccer Teams that captured World Cup titles in 1991 and 1999 and Olympic gold medals in 1996 and 2004. The team's success during her 15-year career made her a hero to countless young girls and launched a continuing wave of interest and participation in women's soccer. Of all the great players on the American team, Foudy emerged as the most prominent spokesperson for her team and ambassador for her sport over the years. In addition, her work outside of soccer on behalf of human rights and civil rights causes has made her a role model for all young women.

Making the U.S. National Team

Foudy's long and storied career with the U.S. National Women's Soccer Team started while she was still in high school. Throughout her years at Mission Viejo High, Foudy had continued to play with the Soccerettes traveling team and also participated in the Olympic Development Program. This program selected the best soccer players from across the country and allowed them to compete at the state, regional, and national levels. During the summer of 1987 — when Foudy was 16 years old and had just completed her sophomore year of high school — she was selected to play on the California Under-19 (U-19) girls' soccer team.

After playing two weeks of tournaments with the California squad, Foudy was promoted to the West Regional U-19 team. When that team's competitions concluded, she was asked to stay and join the national U-19 team for a tournament in Minnesota. To the surprise of many observers, that talented young team ended up doing better than the current U.S. Women's National Soccer Team in the competition, advancing all the way to the finals against Sweden. Afterward, National Team Coach Anson Dorrance chose four of the impressive teenaged players from the national U-19 team — Foudy, Mia Hamm, Kristine Lilly, and Joy Fawcett — to join the U.S. National Women's Soccer Team. These four players transformed the American team into a major force in international competition and became huge stars in the world of soccer. In fact, Grant Wahl of *Sports Illustrated* called Dorrance's 1987 decision "the most important move in U.S. women's soccer history."

Foudy was amazed, after six weeks of competition, to suddenly find herself on the top women's soccer team in the nation. "It was like this unobtainable goal. I didn't realize that I had the potential to play for the national team until that summer. It kind of blew me away, it was so quick. I really didn't have time to think about whether I could play at that level or not," she remembered. "I left a month and a half earlier from home, just thinking I was going to regional camp for two weeks. It just kept going. I kept calling in, 'Mom, Dad, I need more money, I have another camp.' And they were like, 'Whatever, OK, have fun.'"

Playing in the Inaugural Women's World Cup

Foudy made her first appearance in a game as a member of the U.S. national team in 1988, at the age of 17. She continued to play with the team during the summers throughout her years at Stanford. In 1991 she had an opportunity to play in the first-ever FIFA Women's World Cup Championship. The World Cup has been one of the premier events in men's soccer since the early 20th century. Countries around the world form national teams composed of their best players. These teams compete in a series of qualifying matches, and the top teams advance to the World Cup tournament, which takes place every four years. The men's World Cup is the most popular sporting event in the world, so when women's soccer increased in popularity through the 1980s, FIFA decided to hold an equivalent tournament for women.

The 1991 Women's World Cup tournament was held in China. The American team played well, defeating Sweden, Brazil, Japan, Taiwan, and Germany by a cumulative score of 23-4. Foudy played every minute of every game. In the finals, she and her teammates faced a tough team from Norway. The rivals played an exciting match in front of a record crowd of 65,000. In the end, the Americans claimed a 2-1 victory. Foudy was thrilled to capture the inaugural Women's World Cup title. "When we started the team, we never thought there would be a World Cup," she acknowledged. "It was always a mystical thing. And now we're holding it."

> *"When we started the team, we never thought there would be a World Cup,"* Foudy acknowledged. *"It was always a mystical thing. And now we're holding it."*

Unfortunately, the accomplishments of the women's soccer team were largely ignored in the United States, which at that time was not as interested in soccer as the rest of the world. "No one was at the airport to greet us," Foudy remembered. "You'd think that maybe five newspapers would have noticed what we did. I really felt let down. It was like, we got so much out of it personally, but we had no one to share it with. We thought winning the first World Cup was a huge leap for our sport, but it was only a baby step."

Foudy's service to the U.S. national team continued while she graduated from college and was accepted to medical school. In 1995 she deferred her admission in order to help the American women defend their World Cup title. This time, however, Norway got the best of Foudy and her teammates, holding them scoreless in the semifinals and forcing them to settle for a bronze medal. Foudy was deeply disappointed by her team's performance. "I was disgusted with myself," she said afterward. "I felt like I had failed, I had let the team down. I made a promise to myself that I would never let that happen again, ever! Then the whole team gathered right there on the field and made a vow that if we ever got in this position again, we would win!"

> ——— " ———
>
> "This was all that I had dreamed and a hundred times better," Foudy said after winning the gold medal at the 1996 Olympics. "I want to remember this feeling every day."
>
> ——— " ———

Winning Gold at the 1996 Olympics

In 1996 Foudy deferred her medical school admission for a second time. The International Olympic Committee had decided to include women's soccer as a medal sport at the 1996 Summer Games in Atlanta, Georgia, and Foudy jumped at the chance to represent the United States in the Olympics. The U.S. team entered the Games as one of the favorites to win the gold medal, and they quickly proved that they were a force to be reckoned with. In the first two games, they trounced Denmark 3-0 and defeated Sweden by a 2-1 score. The team then fought China, another highly regarded squad, to a 0-0 tie. The 2-0-1 record posted by the U.S. women in the preliminary round enabled the team to advance to the semifinals, where they faced Norway for the right to play in the gold medal match. Foudy and her teammates managed to avenge their World Cup defeat by beating Norway 2-1 in a tense overtime struggle.

The gold medal match pitted the American women against China, the same team they had battled to a scoreless tie earlier in the tournament. A huge crowd of 76,000 people — the largest crowd ever to watch a women's sporting event — turned out for the contest. The two teams treated the crowd to an intense game. The score was tied at 1-1 after 68 minutes of play when America's Tiffeny Milbrett broke through for what ended up being the game-winning goal. The U.S. women played outstanding defense for the remaining 20 minutes of play and held on to earn the gold

Foudy and teammates trounced Denmark, 3-0, in 1996 Olympic competition.

medal. "This was all that I had dreamed and a hundred times better," Foudy said afterward. "I want to remember this feeling every day."

After the exciting gold medal match concluded, Foudy and her teammates were disappointed to learn that the television network that broadcast the Games had not showed it nationally. Instead, the network had only aired a few minutes of highlights. But it turned out to be enough to win the American team and the sport of women's soccer a number of new fans. "It's wild to see people so affected by our sport," Foudy noted. "We've gone from no one but diehard soccer fans knowing who we are to getting cheers from strangers on the street."

Expressing Her Social Conscience

The growing popularity of women's soccer brought Foudy several endorsement opportunities. In 1997, for instance, the major sporting goods producer Reebok asked her to promote a new model of soccer ball.

Around this time, basketball star Michael Jordan and several other professional athletes had received negative publicity for endorsing athletic apparel and equipment that had been made in developing nations using child labor. In some countries, very young children were forced to work long hours for only pennies per day to make gear that sold for top dollar in the United States and Europe.

———— **"** ————

When Foudy was offered an endorsement deal on a new soccer ball, she checked into overseas working conditions. "The kids have to work for the family to survive," Foudy explained. "And when they're working, then they're not getting an education. It becomes a vicious cycle: The kids are working and not being educated, and then they grow up and their kids have to work for the family to survive, and so on."

———— **"** ————

Foudy recalled seeing a documentary film about the making of soccer balls. Regulation balls consist of 32 pieces of leather that are sewn together by hand using over 600 stitches. In many cases, Foudy learned, adults would pick up the supplies for stitching soccer balls at a central location and take them home. Due to the extreme poverty in the areas where the balls were manufactured, the adults would often enlist the help of the entire family—including young children—in sewing the balls together. "The kids have to work for the family to survive," Foudy explained. "And when they're working, then they're not getting an education. It becomes a vicious cycle: The kids are working and not being educated, and then they grow up and their kids have to work for the family to survive, and so on."

Recognizing the potential problems in soccer ball production, Foudy was reluctant to sign a contract with Reebok. Before she agreed to promote the new ball, she insisted on visiting Reebok's factory herself to observe working conditions and ensure that child labor was not exploited in making the product. "If I was going to be a spokesperson for the ball, I wanted to see with my own eyes how the balls are made, rather than hear about it from a million miles away," she stated. "It just makes me crazy when a great athlete is asked about the manufacturing of a product he endorses, and he says, 'I don't know anything about that.'"

Foudy flew to Pakistan and then drove four hours on dirt roads to reach the Reebok factory in Sialkot, a poor village in the foothills of the

*Foudy scores as Mia Hamm runs in for backup
in this 1999 World Cup game.*

Himalayas. "We went into villages and drove through towns, and people would be stitching balls everywhere," she remembered. "It's a huge part of the culture. I never realized how vast it is. Ninety-five percent of the world's soccer balls are made there." Foudy spent three days in Sialkot talking with villagers, playing soccer with children, and assuring herself that Reebok was not exploiting child labor. To her surprise, her trip to Pakistan became national news in the United States. "I just wanted to try to do something to help," she noted. "I had no idea it would be such a big deal to the media. All I know is, I'll never look at a ball the same way again." In 1998 Foudy received FIFA's prestigious Fair Play Award for her work in the realm of human rights. She was the first woman and first American to be so honored.

Winning the 1999 Women's World Cup

In 1998 Foudy served as an analyst for television broadcasts of the men's World Cup soccer tournament. She took the responsibility seriously—studying films and rosters of all the national teams for weeks ahead of time—and received rave reviews for her performance. The following year Foudy appeared in her third Women's World Cup tournament as a player. After the U.S. National Women's Soccer Team won the Olympic gold medal in Atlanta in 1996, women's soccer soared in popularity across the

United States. As a result, there was a great deal of excitement surrounding the 1999 Women's World Cup, which was being held in the United States for the first time.

The tournament featured 16 teams from around the world. These teams played a total of 32 matches over a three-week period in stadiums around the United States. Each team played three games in the opening round, then the top teams advanced through the semifinals and finals. The American team won its first game of the opening round against Denmark, 3-0, in front of a record crowd of 79,000 fans. Foudy and her teammates went on to beat Nigeria, 7-1, and Korea, 3-0, to remain undefeated in opening-round action.

After beating Brazil, 2-0, in the semifinals, the American women went on to the finals at the Rose Bowl in Pasadena, California. They ended up facing China, their rivals from the 1996 Olympic gold medal match, in front of another record crowd of 90,000 fans. The World Cup championship was a tight contest between two evenly matched teams. In fact, the teams went through 90 minutes of regulation play and two 15-minute overtime periods without scoring a single goal. To break the 0-0 tie and decide the winner, a penalty-kick shootout was held.

The United States and China each selected five players to face the opposing goaltender one-on-one. The offensive players line up so close to the goal that they enjoy a significant advantage in these situations and usually score. All five shooters scored for the American team, but U.S. goalkeeper Brianna Scurry made a key save against China's third shooter. The U.S. National Women's Soccer Team thus claimed a dramatic, 5-4 overtime win and their second Women's World Cup championship. More than 41 million people watched the American team's triumph on television, bringing huge numbers of new fans to the sport.

Settling for Silver at the 2000 Olympics

The U.S. Women's National Team had little time to savor their World Cup win. Foudy and her teammates immediately began preparing to defend their Olympic gold medal at the 2000 Games in Sydney, Australia. The American women were widely considered to be the favorites in the Olympics. They went undefeated in international competition leading up to the Games, and they were the defending World Cup champions. In their opening match, the U.S. women faced Norway—the only national team with a winning record against them—and emerged with a 2-0 win.

The American team advanced through the opening round and defeated China in the semifinals. The gold medal match ended up being a rematch between the United States and Norway. The United States scored an early goal, but Norway came back strong and held a 2-1 lead as regulation time expired. In soccer, however, the officials sometimes decide to extend play to make up for stoppages earlier in the game. In the gold medal match, they added 15 seconds to the clock. The U.S. team launched a quick offensive attack during the extra time. Tiffeny Milbrett took a pass from Mia Hamm and headed it into Norway's goal to tie the game and force overtime. Unfortunately, the Americans were unable to achieve a storybook ending. Norway scored 12 minutes into overtime to win the gold medal, and the U.S. had to settle for the silver. (For more in-

Foudy (right) and Mia Hamm (left) react after they lose to Norway at the 2000 Olympics.

formation on Mia Hamm, see *Biography Today Sports,* Vol. 2, and Update in *Biography Today Annual Cumulation,* 2000; for more information on Tiffeny Milbrett, see *Biography Today Sports,* Vol. 10.)

Following the 2000 Games, Foudy helped launch the Women's United Soccer Association (WUSA), an eight-team women's professional soccer league. She played for the San Diego Spirit for the next two seasons, serving as team captain and making the all-WUSA second team both years. As the league prepared for the 2003 season, however, Foudy was shocked to hear that the WUSA was ceasing operations because of financial problems. "This is a sad day for women's soccer and women's sports," she stated. "But we are not just going to give up, even though the odds are stacked against us. We will still hold out the possibility of reviving this." Foudy served as a player representative on the WUSA Reorganization Committee, which was charged with finding a way to revive the league.

Defending Title IX

In 2003 Foudy traveled to Washington, D.C., to serve on the 15-member President's Commission on Opportunity in Athletics. The commission's work involved evaluating proposed changes to Title IX, the landmark 1971 legislation that had increased women's participation in school sports.

Critics argued that, in some cases, Title IX had decreased athletic opportunities for men. Some schools with small athletic budgets had chosen to ensure that men's and women's teams received equal funding by cutting men's teams. After several weeks of heated discussions, 13 members of the commission released a report recommending several changes to Title IX.

Throughout the commission's work, Foudy and two-time Olympic swimming gold medalist Donna de Varona had emerged as the leading voices of protest against these proposed changes. They refused to sign the official report and instead issued a minority report arguing that Title IX was effective and should be maintained in its current form. "Donna de Varona and I both felt there wasn't an alternative voice given in the report they signed off on," Foudy explained. "So we had to write our own, because there was some strong opposition to some of the recommendations they were putting forward. We felt that a handful of them considerably weakened Title IX, and we didn't want to see that happen."

Many people expressed admiration for Foudy's courage in expressing her beliefs about the importance of Title IX. "We knew she was going to be a great soccer player," said U.S. National Team Coach April Heinrichs. "I'm not sure we all knew just how profoundly Julie Foudy would lead this country in terms of sports and this legislation so that it continues to have an impact in young women's lives."

Foudy held a press conference on the steps of the U.S. Capitol building to discuss her position on the issue and her differences with the commission's findings. She and de Varona also appeared on television news programs and were interviewed for newspapers. Their arguments generated a huge response from female athletes, who bombarded U.S. Secretary of Education Rod Paige with e-mails supporting Title IX. Thanks in part to the public outcry, Paige later announced that he intended to ignore the commission's official findings and recommend that no changes be made to Title IX.

Foudy admitted that it was difficult for her to hold a minority position on the commission. "On [the U.S. National Team], we've fought as a voice together. There's always strength in numbers," she explained. "What I discovered on the commission is the courage to still have a voice when you don't have the numbers behind you." Many people expressed admiration for Foudy's courage in expressing her beliefs. "We knew she was going to be a great soccer player," said U.S. National Team Coach April Heinrichs. "I'm not sure we all knew just how profoundly Julie Foudy would lead this country in terms of sports and this legislation so that it continues to have an impact in young women's lives."

Facing Disappointment at the 2003 World Cup

Shortly after her Title IX victory, Foudy returned to the national team to play in the 2003 Women's World Cup. The defending champion United States entered the tournament as one of the favorites to win it all. Armed with a blend of veteran leaders like Foudy and Hamm and young stars such as Aly Wagner, the team expressed confidence that they would be able to make another title run. In the early rounds of the tournament, which was played in the United States, the American squad rolled over the opposition. The team easily advanced to the quarterfinals, where they narrowly defeated Norway 1-0 in a tough, tense match.

In the semifinal match against Germany, however, the U.S. team's dream of a second consecutive World Cup title came to an end. The American squad was shut out 3-0 by the Germans, who played a terrific all-around game. "You're just sitting there by yourself thinking, playing back plays, what we could have done," Foudy lamented afterward. "All the different scenarios." Germany thus advanced to the finals, where they defeated Sweden 2-1 to earn the World Cup title. The loss to Germany was a tremendous disappointment to Foudy and her teammates, but a few days later they rallied to claim third place in the World Cup with a 3-1 victory over Canada.

Going Out with a Bang

Following the disappointment of the 2003 World Cup, the U.S. National Women's Soccer Team appeared to be in turmoil. It marked the first time since women's soccer had become an Olympic sport that the American team did not hold either the World Cup or Olympic title. As the team prepared for the 2004 Olympic Games in Athens, Greece, several players complained about the coaching or expressed concern about the team's ability to blend veteran talents with rising young stars. Leading up to the Games, however, several of the team's original stars—including Foudy, Mia Hamm, and Joy Fawcett—announced their decision to retire following the Olympic tournament. The team then seemed to come together around the desire to give these legendary players a memorable send-off.

The American women advanced through the tournament to qualify for the medal round. They beat Germany 2-1 in overtime in the semifinals,

Foudy (left) celebrating the U.S. team's 2004 Olympic gold medal win with her teammates, Mia Hamm (center) and Kristine Lilly (right).

despite the fact that Foudy suffered a sprained right ankle that limited her playing time. The Americans faced an exciting young team from Brazil in the gold medal match. Foudy came back from her injury to play the entire game, which saw the U.S. team prevail 2-1 in overtime. Foudy was thrilled to cap her remarkable career with a second Olympic gold medal.

Even though she was excited about pursuing new opportunities in retirement, Foudy acknowledged that she would miss playing soccer. "Soccer is such a fun sport to play, and it's so healthy to play it. Any boy or girl who develops an interest in soccer is a lucky boy or girl. And how lucky I am, how truly lucky, to get to be a part of that," she stated. "What I preach to young kids is if you really want to be successful, you really have to have that hunger, that love, that competitive fire to get to the next level, and there's no complacency."

For her next career, Foudy has considered going into sports broadcasting or possibly politics. A number of prominent people have expressed their support for this idea. "Certain personalities come along at certain times in history, and her timing is correct and she's the one," said tennis legend Billie Jean King, another prominent spokesperson for women in sports. "She's got the gift. She wants to make a positive difference and maybe take another step forward for all of us."

MARRIAGE AND FAMILY

Foudy met her future husband, soccer coach Ian Sawyers, in 1989—the year she graduated from high school. Although Sawyers was quite a bit older, she was attracted by his passion for soccer and his British accent. They dated throughout her years at Stanford and were married on July 30, 1995.

Foudy admits that her busy travel schedule with the U.S. national team sometimes made it tricky to devote time to her marriage. "It's not easy or ideal, but it's doable," she once said. "The first component is to have a wonderful husband who supports what you're doing. Ian is phenomenal. He's never once said, 'I don't like this.' He understands the commitment and that it won't last a lifetime." Now that Foudy is retired, she and her husband hope to start a family.

HOBBIES AND OTHER INTERESTS

In her spare time, Foudy enjoys snowboarding, in-line skating, and playing golf. She is also a spokesperson for the TopSoccer program, which creates opportunities for kids with disabilities to play soccer.

——— *"* ———

"Soccer is such a fun sport to play, and it's so healthy to play it. Any boy or girl who develops an interest in soccer is a lucky boy or girl. And how lucky I am, how truly lucky, to get to be a part of that," Foudy stated. "What I preach to young kids is if you really want to be successful, you really have to have that hunger, that love, that competitive fire to get to the next level, and there's no complacency."

HONORS AND AWARDS

——— *"* ———

High School Girls' Soccer All-American: 1987, 1988
Southern California Soccer Player of the Decade (*Los Angeles Times*): 1989
NCAA Freshman of the Year: 1989
NCAA All-American: 1989-92
Soccer America Player of the Year: 1991
FIFA Women's World Cup Championship: 1991, gold medal; 1995, bronze medal; 1999, gold medal; 2003, bronze medal
Olympic Women's Soccer: 1996, gold medal; 2000, silver medal; 2004, gold medal
FIFA Fair Play Award: 1998
Sportswomen of the Year (*Sports Illustrated*): 1999, with other members of the U.S. Women's National Soccer Team

FURTHER READING

Books

Christopher, Matt. *On the Field with Julie Foudy,* 2000
Rutledge, Rachel. *The Best of the Best in Soccer,* 1998
Savage, Jeff. *Julie Foudy: Soccer Superstar,* 1999
Who's Who in America, 2005

Periodicals

Chicago Tribune, May 3, 1997, News, p.1; July 4, 1999, Sports, p.1
Denver Post, Sep. 14, 2003, p.C4
Los Angeles Times, June 25, 1991, p.C1; Apr. 18, 1998, p.C12; June 19, 1999, p.A1
Ms., Summer 2003, p.71
New York Times, June 16, 1999, p.D6
Orange County (CA) Register, Apr. 15, 1996, p.C13; Apr. 24, 1998, p.D9
Philadelphia Inquirer, Sep. 25, 2003, p.E1
Sports Illustrated, June 2, 1997, p.22; June 21, 1999, p.64; Oct. 13, 2003, p.105
Time, July 19, 1999, p.62
USA Today, Sep. 9, 2003, p.C1; Dec. 10, 2004, p.C14
Women's Sports and Fitness, July-Aug. 1998, p.94; July-Aug. 1999, p.75

Online Databases

Biography Resource Center Online, 2005

ADDRESS

Julie Foudy
U.S. Soccer Federation
1801 South Prairie Avenue
Chicago, IL 60616-1319

WORLD WIDE WEB SITE

http://wusa.com

Laird Hamilton 1964-

American Big-Wave Surfer
Pioneered the Tow-In Method of Surfing

BIRTH

Laird Hamilton was born on March 2, 1964, in San Francisco, California. His mother, Joann, gave birth to him in a bathysphere — an experimental birthing chamber designed to reduce the pull of gravity and allow the baby to float freely in the womb — at the University of California Medical Center. Laird's biological father left the family soon after he was born. At the age of two, Laird moved to the Hawaiian island of Oahu, where his mother became a helicopter tour operator.

71

According to family legend, Laird chose his own stepfather shortly after their arrival in Hawaii. The toddler was playing at the beach when he met Bill Hamilton, a world-class surfer. Bill took Laird body surfing and established an immediate bond with the boy. "He had his arms around my neck the whole day, and I could just feel this very deep connection between us," Bill recalled. "He said, 'I want you to be my father,' and we went back [to Laird's house] for dinner, and Joann and I fell in love and eventually got married." The marriage produced another son, Lyon, who is Laird's younger half-brother.

> "One of my first memories [of surfing] was at Lahaina, Maui. I was about two and a half and was pushed out onto a wave. I fell on the urchin bottom and impaled my buttocks with urchins, and I couldn't sit down for two weeks. That left a lasting impression on me, literally."

YOUTH

Growing up on the north shore of Oahu, Laird made the nearby Pacific Ocean a part of his daily life. "I could swim before I could walk and spent my childhood on the beach," he recalled. "By the time I was two, I was balancing on the front of my dad's surfboard. I progressed to my own little board and was always in the warm Pacific." Fearless and daring from an early age, Laird developed a passion for surfing that endured numerous injuries. "One of my first memories [of surfing] was at Lahaina, Maui," he remembered. "I was about two and a half and was pushed out onto a wave. I fell on the urchin bottom and impaled my buttocks with urchins, and I couldn't sit down for two weeks. That left a lasting impression on me, literally."

In 1971 the Hamilton family moved to the remote Wainiha Valley on the Hawaiian island of Kauai. Laird and his brother hunted wild pigs in the rainforest and found countless ways to court danger and get in trouble. When Laird was eight years old, his father took him to a famous 60-foot cliff at Waimea Falls, where daredevils came from far and wide to test their courage. To his father's shock, Laird took one look over the edge and then jumped. "He's been bold since day one, and hell-bent on living life to the extreme," Bill Hamilton noted. Laird remembered his first cliff-jumping experience as an important moment in his life. "I think that was the beginning of my attraction to . . . the whole adrenaline and mental buildup, psyching myself up to do something like that and then actually doing it."

Hamilton at age 10. By that point, he was already riding 12-foot waves.

By the age of 10, Laird was riding 12-foot waves on his surfboard. He also enjoyed other sports, like windsurfing, and often sailed across the 70 miles of open ocean between the islands of Maui and Oahu. His daring nature made him so unconcerned about the risk of injury that he stopped counting the number of stitches he received when the total reached 1,000.

By the time he was 14, Laird's surfing abilities rivaled those of his father, who was a star on the Association of Surfing Professionals' World Championship Tour for many years. But Laird never took part in professional surfing competitions. He had seen the pain his father endured due to the whims of contest judges, and he came to view surfing as an art form that should not be subjected to arbitrary judging. "[My father] was one of the most beautiful of surfers, but his whole happiness was fluttering on the wings of a few judges," he recalled. "It was devastating. Financially, trying to feed a family, but also not getting due respect because you won't dance the way they want you to dance. . . . I vowed never to subject myself to that."

EDUCATION

Hamilton attended Kapaa High School in Kauai, where he was one of only a few Caucasian students. His Pacific Islander classmates called him "haole," an unkind word for white person, and he got in numerous fist-fights. "Girls liked me, but their brothers and cousins would not let them go out with me," he remembered. Hamilton dropped out of high school at the age of 16 in order to pursue a career in surfing.

CAREER HIGHLIGHTS

Launching a Career in Water Sports

Since he rejected the competition circuit, Hamilton had to find another way to make a living through surfing. After quitting school, he started out doing construction work. At 17 he was discovered on a Kauai beach by a photographer for the Italian magazine *L'Uomo Vogue* (Men's Vogue). He then embarked on a brief modeling career that included a photo shoot with actress-model Brooke Shields in 1983. The following year Hamilton moved to Los Angeles to promote a fashion line of surfwear, but he soon grew frustrated with the modeling business. "Modeling became the last thing in the world I wanted to do," he acknowledged. "I felt like a creature on display. Good looks don't make you a good person — it's inside that counts." Hamilton also longed to get out of the hectic big city and return to the casual, ocean-focused world of his youth. "I felt my gills drying up," he noted. "My whole youth was being wasted."

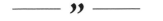

> "*Modeling became the last thing in the world I wanted to do,*" Hamilton acknowledged. "*I felt like a creature on display. Good looks don't make you a good person — it's inside that counts.*"

In 1986 Hamilton left Los Angeles and entered a speed-sailing competition in Port Saint-Louis, France. He defeated the heavily favored French champion, Pascal Maka, and broke the European speed record of 36 knots. His success in this event led to a contract to travel around the world promoting sailboard accessories. The financial security this contract provided gave Hamilton the freedom to try out a variety of water sports. He stroked the famous 26-mile Hawaiian canoe racecourse from Molokai to Oahu on a paddleboard, for example, and also crossed the English Channel on a surfboard.

Hamilton in action at Tunnels, Kauai, 1984.

In the early 1990s Hamilton joined a group of eight surfer friends from Maui to form the Strapt crew, which became known for its water-sports innovations and daring feats. They experimented with "connected" surfing — using Velcro to attach their feet to the surfboard — which allowed them to perform aerial tricks on the waves. They also surfed waves using sailboards and attracted the attention of TV and film crews by launching 30-foot jumps. Finally, the group experimented with a combination of surfing and paragliding to develop one of the earliest forms of kiteboarding.

Towing into the Big Waves

Hamilton and the other members of the Strapt crew eventually turned their attention to "big-wave surfing," or devising ways to ride the monster waves of 20 feet or more that occasionally reached Hawaii as a result of winter storms in the Pacific. The largest wave ever surfed up to that time was a 35-footer ridden by the legendary Greg Noll in Hawaii in 1969 — and Noll scared himself so badly that he gave up surfing a short time later. Many accomplished surfers tried to beat the record over the years, but none were successful. "It was like there was a ceiling, around 25 feet," Hamilton acknowledged. "Big-wave surfing was stuck in a rut. It was not getting the respect or attention that it deserved."

Hamilton watched hours of videotape footage showing surfers wiping out on huge waves. He noticed that the traditional method of surfing—in which the surfer lies face-down on the board and paddles with the arms before standing up to ride the wave—could not generate enough speed to catch the big waves, which often travel at upwards of 30 miles per hour. He decided that an innovative new approach was needed, and that his childhood experiences made him uniquely qualified to develop one. "Growing up in Hawaii, and growing up with the Hawaiians, you ride waves with canoes and sailboards," he explained. "You body surf and knee board. When you look at surfing like that—there's so many ways to ride a wave—it opens your mind up to new ways to do it. That open-minded thinking was the basis for all the things that happened."

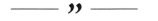

> "Growing up in Hawaii, and growing up with the Hawaiians, you ride waves with canoes and sailboards," Hamilton explained. "You body surf and knee board. When you look at surfing like that—there's so many ways to ride a wave—it opens your mind up to new ways to do it. That open-minded thinking was the basis for all the things that happened."

In 1992 Hamilton and his friends decided to use motorized boats to tow one another into the path of big waves. They started out using tiny inflatable Zodiac boats and later graduated to speedy, maneuverable personal watercraft (often known as jet skis). The surfer would stand on a specially designed surfboard and hold on to a waterski tow rope. The boat would match the speed of the wave, and then the surfer would let go of the rope and ride it. Although some surfing purists claimed that tow-in surfing was cheating, Hamilton dismissed this idea. He pointed out that the Hawaiian kings who originated the sport had used mechanical assistance, leaping from outrigger canoes paddled by dozens of men in order to catch big offshore waves.

Conquering "Jaws"

Hamilton spent his boyhood surfing just up the coast from "Jaws," an infamous spot on the north shore of Maui that regularly generates 40- to 50-foot waves. The coastline in that area consists of sheer rocky cliffs, and the nearest launching point for surfers is three miles away. Although many

Hamilton surfing at Jaws, with a rescue helicopter hovering nearby.

surfers looked down longingly at the massive breakers, Jaws was always considered too dangerous to surf. But in 1993, using the new tow-in method of surfing, Hamilton became the first person to conquer Jaws. Afterward, he claimed that approaching the huge break while standing up gave him a whole different perspective. "All these years we've been looking at the waves from a worm's perspective," he noted. "When you're lying down, looking up at them, the waves appear huge and threatening. With tow-surfing, you're looking at waves from a human perspective. What this has done is just raise the top-end limit."

Over the next decade, Hamilton became the most prominent athlete in the emerging sport of big-wave surfing. As he conquered ever bigger and more dangerous waves, his triumphs inspired other daring surfers, leading to a worldwide competition to ride the biggest wave ever. "The waves he surfs for a living are too large to describe," Jeff MacGregor wrote in *Sports Illustrated*. "A city block in mid-Manhattan conveys the scale of one of these things, the breadth and the tonnage, but not its evil velocity or murderous intentions. These are great, fat, 50-foot growlers that travel thousands of miles to lift you up, fill your spirit with giddy music of the spheres, and then kill you."

Hamilton surfing at Teahupoo in Tahiti.

"Sure, if you make a mistake, the consequences could be fatal," Hamilton admitted. "It's impossible not to be afraid. Fear is an intricate part of respect for the ocean, and to know and understand its strength you have to fear it. It's one of our most powerful emotions, and fear of death is what makes us struggle to survive. I use my fear as energy and as a power source to motivate me." Hamilton claimed that the thrill of riding a huge wave more than compensated for the risk involved. "When you're riding that huge wave, you feel as if you're flying," he explained. "You have the freedom of flight without the sensation of falling. It's absolutely amazing because you are carried, literally, on the crest of a wave."

Gaining Fame and Fortune

Hamilton's success in conquering Jaws helped him win a high-profile sponsorship from Oxbow, a French beachwear company, in 1994. It also led to an appearance on the cable-television sports channel ESPN and a spot on the cover of *Outside* magazine. In 1996 Hamilton was named to *People* magazine's list of the 50 Most Beautiful People in the World. That same year, he made headlines by leaving his first wife, Maria Souza, and moving in with professional volleyball player and model Gabrielle Reece. The two athletes were married in 1997. Hamilton also joined Reece as a host of the cable-TV sports series "The Extremists," and in 2000 he hosted the "Planet Extreme Championships" on the Fox Sports Network.

Meanwhile, Hamilton continued accomplishing extreme feats of his own. In 2001 he became the first person ever to surf a dangerous break called Teahupoo in Tahiti. He rode a giant wave that was breaking in just a few feet of water over a razor-sharp reef. His performance at Teahupoo was named Feat of the Year at ESPN's Action Sports and Music Awards. It also led to an opportunity for him to perform surfing stunts in the 2002 James Bond movie *Die Another Day*.

Hamilton has appeared in several surfing-related films over the years, including 1994's *Endless Summer II* and the successful 2003 documentary *Step into Liquid*. In 2004 he starred in the documentary *Riding Giants*, which traces the history of big-wave surfing from its Polynesian roots to Hamilton's quest to ride a perfect 100-footer. The film also features Greg Noll and Laird's father, Bill Hamilton. "One of my objectives in the beginning was to really try to create a film that would help strengthen the image of surfers and just kind of let people know how dedicated we are and how professional we are," Hamilton said. "It's the kind of film I always wanted to see about surfing. It's the real story about the real people." A reviewer for *Los Angeles Magazine* called *Riding Giants* "a glorious film, at its best when capturing the spectacle of ant-sized humans getting pounded by waves that stretch end to end across the screen."

> **"**
>
> *"The waves he surfs for a living are too large to describe," Jeff MacGregor wrote in* **Sports Illustrated.** *"A city block in mid-Manhattan conveys the scale of one of these things, the breadth and the tonnage, but not its evil velocity or murderous intentions. These are great, fat, 50-foot growlers that travel thousands of miles to lift you up, fill your spirit with giddy music of the spheres, and then kill you."*
>
> **"**

Hamilton decided to capitalize on his success in the movie industry by forming his own film production company, BamMan Productions, in 2003. His company produced a TV pilot called "The Ride," which won the Best Film award at the X-Dance Action Sports Festival in Park City, Utah.

Hamilton hoped to turn the pilot into an extreme-sports reality-TV series. His company was also involved in producing an Imax film about big-wave surfing for Disney.

Becoming a Legend

Hamilton is often referred to as the greatest big-wave surfer of all time. He has achieved legendary status in his sport despite his consistent refusal to compete in traditional surfing contests. "I don't like man-against-man competition," he stated. "I'm man against the elements." Hamilton has even refused to enter his big-wave rides into the record books, preferring instead to ride for his own satisfaction. "You'll never hear from me, 'I rode the biggest wave,'" he declared. "Because you hurt yourself by saying, 'This is it.' Like a benchmark. Then people want to step over that. For me, it's less about the one big wave than about your performances. It's about your body of work. It's art."

———— **"** ————

"When you're riding that huge wave, you feel as if you're flying," Hamilton explained. "You have the freedom of flight without the sensation of falling. It's absolutely amazing because you are carried, literally, on the crest of a wave."

———— **"** ————

Hamilton is also legendary for his workout regimen, which might include riding up mountainsides with 50 pounds strapped to his bike, harnessing himself to a log and dragging it for miles down the beach, or paddling a surfboard for miles across the open ocean. "If I can get three or four activities in during a day, I can sleep well, and food tastes better," he explained.

Although Hamilton has suffered numerous injuries over the years—he has broken his left ankle five times, for example—he plans to continue training and surfing big waves for a long time. "When I'm 60, I hope that I'll be training harder than I've ever been," he stated. "I want to continue to keep focused on keeping the car running. Keep it moving. I've never been in better condition. . . . You can surf until you're buried."

Despite the risks involved, Hamilton insists that big-wave surfing provides him with a sense of peace. "What I love is the silent beauty of the moment," he noted. "Me alone with the elements, not fighting nature but just tucking in alongside her. Riding a glassy 60-foot wave, mowing up and down the face in perfect synch like it was a 6-foot shore break, and then

Hamilton in action, 2005.

just turning away and letting it go on its way untamed and unsullied. Perfect peace, a moment stolen from heaven, a place where nobody else has been and can never go again because seconds later the wave has broken and exists only in my memory."

But even though he receives the ultimate satisfaction from big-wave surfing, Hamilton warns inexperienced surfers not to try to imitate him. "Don't try it at home, kids, or not yet anyway," he stated. "Work up to the big waves slowly. You need a lifetime of experience to be safe out there. The good news is that the big waves have been breaking for tens of thousands of years and will go on breaking for eternity. You have a lifetime to get it right. Aloha."

MARRIAGE AND FAMILY

Hamilton met his first wife, Maria Souza, a Brazilian clothing designer and former gymnast, while bodyboarding on Waimea Bay. They had a daughter together, Izabela, before the marriage ended in divorce. Hamilton met former professional volleyball player and model Gabrielle Reece in 1995, when she interviewed him for an extreme-sports television show. They were married in November 30, 1997, in a canoe on the

Hanalei River in Maui. They have a daughter, Reece Viola Hamilton, who was born in October 2003.

Hamilton and his wife Gabrielle spend the winter surfing season in Hawaii. In 2004 they started building a 3,500-square-foot house in Haiku, Maui, just up the road from the surf break known as Jaws. They spend the summer traveling or in California, where they own a 10,000-square-foot Mediterranean-style mansion in Malibu.

Hamilton claims that his wife supports his passion for surfing. "She'd prefer the ocean be the 'other woman' rather than there really being another woman in my life," he explained. Although he takes his daughter Reece to the ocean every day, he says that he will let her decide whether she wants to surf. "I want to expose her to a multitude of activities and let her choose," he noted. "That way she'll enjoy it and be fulfilled."

> ———— " ————
>
> *"What I love is the silent beauty of the moment,"* Hamilton noted. *"Me alone with the elements, not fighting nature but just tucking in alongside her. Riding a glassy 60-foot wave, mowing up and down the face in perfect synch like it was a 6-foot shore break, and then just turning away and letting it go on its way untamed and unsullied. Perfect peace, a moment stolen from heaven, a place where nobody else has been and can never go again because seconds later the wave has broken and exists only in my memory."*
>
> ———— " ————

HOBBIES AND OTHER INTERESTS

When he is not in the water or training on land, Hamilton enjoys spending time in his workshop designing and building new kinds of equipment for water sports. "I really want to be an inventor," he explained. "I dig that whole process, from idea to prototype." One of his latest innovations is an airboard—a short surfboard with a hydrofoil wing attached to the bottom to provide lift, which increases speed and stability in choppy water. "These new boards are unbelievable," he stated. "We ride on the foil itself. It's like a little airplane underwater. It has a fuselage and two wings. It has this long fin, almost three feet long. So the whole board flies above the water. It allows us to ride waves that don't break. We can catch the waves substantially further out in the ocean and ride them even if they don't break for long periods of time. It's going to create a new dimension and way to ride the ocean. It will create an opportunity to go places that were not looked at for surfing." Hamilton is also considering trying out for the Greek bobsled team (his biological father was Greek) that will compete in the 2006 Olympic Games.

SELECTED CREDITS

Films

Radical Attitude, 1992
Endless Summer II, 1994
Wake Up Call, 1996
Laird, 2001
Step into Liquid, 2003
Riding Giants, 2004

Television

"The Extremists," 1996-97 (host)
"Planet Extreme Championships," 2000 (host)
"The Ride," 2003 (producer and host)

HONORS AND AWARDS

Breakout Performance of the Year (Surfer Poll Awards): 2000
Feat of the Year (ESPN Action Sports and Music Awards): 2001
Surfers' Hall of Fame: 2002

FURTHER READING

Periodicals

Baltimore Sun, Nov. 29, 2004, p.D1
Daily Telegraph (London), May 10, 2004, Sport, p.7
Fort Worth Star-Telegram, July 14, 2004, p.D2
Independent (London), Apr. 26, 2001, p.24
Los Angeles Magazine, Aug. 2004, p.67
Mirror (London), Apr. 7, 2001, p.6
New York Post, July 4, 2004, p.84
Outside, June 1994, p.76; Dec. 2004, p.83
People, May 22, 2000, p.77
Sports Illustrated, Mar. 22, 1999, p.22; Feb. 25, 2000, p.142

ADDRESS

Laird Hamilton
Jane Kachmer Management
5111 Ocean Front Walk, Suite 4
Marina Del Ray, CA 90292

WORLD WIDE WEB SITE

http://www.lairdhamilton.com

Betty Lennox 1976-

American Basketball Player with the Seattle Storm
2000 WNBA Rookie of the Year and 2004 WNBA
Finals Most Valuable Player

BIRTH

Betty Bernice Lennox was born in Hugo, Oklahoma, on December 4, 1976. She was the eighth of nine children born to Bernice Lennox. Betty has five brothers—Freddy, Karl, A.B., Alfred, and Charles—and three sisters—Lela, Ruby, and Victoria.

YOUTH

Betty Lennox was raised on a farm outside of the small town of Hugo. She and her siblings got up early every morning to do chores, such as hauling hay, picking cotton, and tending cows. Their mother depended on their labor to help support the family. "That was money that put food on our table," Betty explained. "We'd always ask my mom when we were going to get paid and she always said, 'When you sit down and eat supper, that's your paycheck.'"

Betty loved the game of basketball from an early age. One year she even dressed up as a basketball for Halloween. She grew up playing on a dirt court, using a hoop made out of an old bicycle rim. She usually competed against her five older brothers and their friends. They only allowed her to play on the condition that she not expect to receive any special treatment on account of her age, size, or gender. "My brothers taught me: 'Don't be scared of anything,'" she noted. "I go into games and don't get intimidated by anyone."

Betty has said that her childhood experiences helped make her tough. "I was raised in a tough household—very poor—and fought for everything that I got. I was raised not to take anything lightly," she recalled. "I wasn't necessarily wild, but I liked to fight a lot. I had a short temper and a bad attitude."

EDUCATION

Lennox attended the public schools in Hugo as a girl. She started playing organized basketball in junior high. At that time, Oklahoma was one of the last states in the country to require girls to play an old-fashioned, half-court version of the game. Each team consisted of six players—three on offense and three on defense. Neither offensive nor defensive players were allowed to cross the line at center court. Lennox played offense and developed her talents as a scorer. "I was scoring 60 points every game I played," she remembered. "I never had to worry about defense. Just dribble and shoot, dribble and shoot. It's what God made me to do."

When Lennox was in ninth grade, however, she moved to Independence, Missouri. During tryouts for the varsity basketball team at Fort Osage High School, she did not realize that she could run the length of the court. "When I dribbled the ball to half-court, I stopped," she recalled. "I didn't think I could cross. Everybody was laughing at me. I was like, Is there something on my pants?" Lennox soon adapted to regulation basketball and learned to play defense.

Lennox went back to Oklahoma for her sophomore year of high school, then returned to Fort Osage for her junior year in 1994. The girls' basketball team posted a 20-8 record that season and claimed the first district championship in school history. During her senior year, Lennox averaged 16.4 points per game and led her team to a 27-1 record and another district championship. She finished her high school career with 1,100 points to become the all-time leading scorer in Fort Osage history. Later, in 2001, the school held a special ceremony to retire her jersey.

Although Lennox worked hard in school, she still struggled academically. When she graduated from Fort Osage in 1995, her grades were not good enough to qualify for a basketball scholarship to a four-year college. Lennox enrolled at nearby Butler Community College in Kansas, but she quickly became dissatisfied with the school's weak women's basketball program. "I knew it was all wrong when I saw our 300-pound, no-muscle post player," she recalled. In 1996 Lennox transferred to Trinity Valley Community College in Athens, Texas. She averaged an impressive 26.4 points per game during her sophomore year and helped lead her team to a 34-2 record and the national junior college women's championship.

Lennox's strong performance on the court helped her earn a basketball scholarship to attend Louisiana Tech, which was a national powerhouse in women's basketball. She entered Louisiana Tech in 1997 but voluntarily took a year off from basketball in order to focus on her studies. "I had to do that to succeed," she stated. "But it was hard not to be playing. I'd go watch the girls practice, and then I'd go to the park to find some guys to play basketball with." Lennox watched

At first, Lennox had trouble adapting from half-court to full-court basketball. "When I dribbled the ball to half-court, I stopped," she recalled. "I didn't think I could cross. Everybody was laughing at me. I was like, Is there something on my pants?"

Lennox celebrating with her Louisiana Tech teammates after winning the Sun Belt Championship, 2000.

from the stands as the Lady Techsters made it all the way to the NCAA Finals that year, losing the national championship game to the University of Tennessee. The year off from basketball enabled Lennox to graduate from Louisiana Tech in 2000 with a bachelor's degree in psychology.

CAREER HIGHLIGHTS

College — The Louisiana Tech Lady Techsters

Upon joining the Lady Techsters for the 1998-99 season, Lennox struggled to adjust to the disciplined style of basketball preferred by Coach Leon Barmore. She grew frustrated at sitting on the bench and earned the nickname "Psycho" for her outbursts of temper. During one game, for example, she became so upset with the quality of her own play that she scrawled "Don't put me back in the game" on the coach's blackboard at halftime. Barmore responded by throwing an eraser across the locker room.

Over time, however, Lennox started to understand that her coach only wanted to make her a better player and a better person. "He sat me over to the side and told me, 'Betty, believe it or not, I'm going to change you before you leave here. The way you act to get your way, you're not going to act that way anymore. You are going to play in my system. You are going to change as a person,'" she remembered.

Lennox gradually took control of her off-court behavior and took out her aggressions on the court instead. She impressed Barmore and her teammates with her hard work, spending hours after practice in the weight room or watching game films. "Inside her gut, every day, she wanted to be good," Barmore said. "When you run across someone like that, you treasure them." Lennox averaged 10 points and 4.2 rebounds per game during her junior year. The Lady Techsters advanced to the Final Four of the NCAA Championship Tournament, where they lost to Purdue.

Lennox cracked the starting lineup at shooting guard as a senior in 1999-2000. She and point guard Tamicha Jackson gave the Lady Techsters one of the best backcourt tandems in the country. Lennox averaged 17.5 points per game to help her team amass an impressive 31-3 record. The Lady Techsters advanced to the quarterfinals of the NCAA Tournament before losing to Penn State. Lennox was named Sun Coast Conference Player of the Year, and she also earned first-team All-American honors from the U.S.A. Basketball Writers Association and the Women's Basketball News Service.

"He sat me over to the side and told me, 'Betty, believe it or not, I'm going to change you before you leave here,'" Lennox said, recalling the advice from Louisiana Tech Coach Leon Barmore. "'The way you act to get your way, you're not going to act that way anymore. You are going to play in my system. You are going to change as a person.'"

WNBA — The Minnesota Lynx

On the strength of her outstanding senior season at Louisiana Tech, Lennox became the sixth player selected in the 2000 WNBA draft. She was chosen by the Minnesota Lynx and looked forward to starting her professional basketball career. When Lennox struggled to adapt to Coach Brian Agler's system, she called her college coach to ask for advice. "I said, 'Look. That guy can coach. Be patient. He has a game plan,'" Barmore recalled.

Lennox took the advice to heart and worked hard to fit in with the Lynx. After averaging only 8.2 points per game for the first four games of the season, she caught fire and more than doubled her average to 16.9 points per game by the end of the season. She also added 5.6 rebounds per game, which was the highest average among all guards in the league. "Rebounding makes her the player she is," said Lynx Coach Brian Agler. "She has great anticipation, is quick off the floor, and is determined to get the ball."

At mid-season Lennox became the only rookie chosen by coaches to play in the 2000 WNBA All-Star Game. "I was surprised," she said. "It's a good feeling. I really have accomplished more than I thought here. It's just a wonderful feeling." Although the Lynx failed to make the playoffs, the team's star shooting guard earned WNBA Rookie of the Year honors for 2000. Lennox was thrilled to receive the award. "When I set the goal [of winning Rookie of the Year honors] I thought it was somewhat out of reach but as the season went along I thought it was more possible," she noted. "I thought that if I put my mind to this and work at it, I could do it."

> "Rebounding makes her the player she is," said Lynx Coach Brian Agler. "She has great anticipation, is quick off the floor, and is determined to get the ball."

Unfortunately, Lennox could not duplicate her outstanding rookie season. In 2001 she suffered an injury to her left hip that caused her to miss 20 games in the middle of the season. She only appeared in 11 games, during which she averaged 11 points and 4.9 rebounds. After aggravating the injury toward the end of the season, she underwent surgery to repair the damage in November 2001.

Lennox spent the next six months recovering from her surgery and trying to learn a new position. Coach Agler asked her to move from shooting guard to point guard for the 2002 season. "It's most definitely not my natural position," she noted. "It takes a lot of concentration, getting yelled at, control, leadership. It's a big challenge." Lennox started at point guard in the Lynx's season opener and had one of the worst games of her career, committing 9 turnovers and missing 17 of 22 shots.

Although Agler had assured Lennox that he would be patient with her adjustment to the point guard position, the coach seemed to lose confidence in her immediately. She was relegated to the bench for the next four games and only contributed 6.2 points and 3.2 rebounds per game. Then, five games into the 2002 season, the Lynx traded Lennox to the Miami Sol.

Lennox playing for the Minnesota Lynx during her outstanding rookie season, 2000.

Lennox was angry about the trade and felt betrayed by her coach. "He conned me into thinking I'd be here for years to come. He made me think he'd allow me to make mistakes at this position and let me get better," she stated. "You don't become a true point guard in a month. I wasn't given a chance. I sacrificed my reputation [as a scorer] for Brian Agler. I stayed and worked eight hours a day for him. He said he never lost confidence in me, and that was a lie."

Bouncing around the League

Despite her hard feelings about the trade, Lennox was determined to return to form in Miami. She came off the bench at shooting guard and provided a spark to her new team. The Sol had struggled to a 1-5 record before the trade but went 8-6 after acquiring Lennox. "I don't think there's any question her addition to our team has helped us dramatically," said Sol Coach Ron Rothstein. Lennox led the team in scoring seven times and ended up averaging 11.9 points and 2.8 rebounds per game during the 2002 season. She started to view the trade as a positive development in her career. "I think the move was great for me," she stated. "I'm just taking advantage of the opportunities I have now."

Unfortunately, the Sol franchise suffered financial problems and the team folded at the end of the year. The WNBA held a special dispersal draft so that other teams could claim the players on the Sol roster. Lennox was selected third in this draft by the Cleveland Rockers. During the off-season, Lennox trained with the USA Basketball Women's Team that would compete in the World Championships. Although she was eventually cut from the team, she attracted the attention of Coach Anne Donovan, who also coached the WNBA's Seattle Storm.

Lennox did not make much of a mark with Cleveland during the 2003 season. She came off the bench and saw limited playing time, only contributing 7.6 points and 2.6 rebounds per game. The Rockers then went out of business at the end of the year, making Lennox the only player in WNBA history to be involved in a dispersal draft in two consecutive seasons.

Many teams seemed to shy away from Lennox in the dispersal draft. Some coaches believed that her hip injury continued to affect her play. Others believed that she had a bad attitude and would be a distraction in the locker room. But Coach Donovan, who knew Lennox from her tryouts with the USA Women's Basketball Team, felt differently. Convinced that Lennox possessed the scoring ability and aggressiveness that the Seattle Storm needed, Donovan selected her with the sixth pick in the dispersal draft. "Betty is an exciting player who adds solid depth to our perimeter game," said Donovan. "She's an explosive shooting guard who has had tremendous success in this league."

In Seattle, Lennox joined a promising young team led by 2003 WNBA Most Valuable Player Lauren Jackson at power forward and emerging star Sue Bird at point guard. The Storm also traded for small forward Sheri Sam and center Janell Burse during the off-season. This solid line-up allowed Lennox to use her strengths as a scoring threat and aggressive defender. "I don't think my focus will be coming in here and scoring," she noted. "Of course you've got the MVP on the team, I just think I will be an addition, able to help out in scoring and do the other dirty work, be the hard-nosed defensive player, the gnat on the team. I think my scoring ability is a plus, but I don't think it will be something that we'll live or die by. Which is going to make me feel comfortable as a player coming in, more relaxed to do what I need to do to participate."

Winning the WNBA Title with the Seattle Storm

Upon joining the Storm for the 2004 season, Lennox felt rejuvenated. "The handcuffs are off," she stated. "There's no being tied down or yanked out of a game because I made a mistake. It's freedom." She responded by turning in her best performance since her rookie season. She started 32 games at shooting guard and averaged 11.2 points, 5.0 rebounds, and 2.5 assists per game. These figures likely would have been higher except that she suffered a broken nose in June, which kept her out of the lineup for two games and required her to wear a protective mask for much of the season. Donovan credited Lennox for giving the Storm an edge that helped them make the playoffs. "Right away she changed the image of the Storm from a talented but nice team," the coach explained. "We wanted to be a more aggressive, nastier team."

> *Lennox possessed the scoring ability and aggressiveness that the Seattle Storm needed, according to Coach Anne Donovan. "Betty is an exciting player who adds solid depth to our perimeter game," said Donovan. "She's an explosive shooting guard who has had tremendous success in this league."*

In Seattle, Lennox also displayed a greater capacity to control her temper and aggressive nature in the locker room while expressing it on the court. "I've grown a lot as a person," she noted. "People who knew me before and who know me now will tell you it's a night-and-day change. Don't base everything on what's been said or written about Betty Lennox. Those people don't know the real me. You've got to judge for yourself about who I am now."

Lennox's coach agreed that she had been a model player for the Storm. "She's worked really hard to craft her game to what our needs are,"

Lennox and Nykesha Sales of the Connecticut Sun battling for control in Game 2 of the WNBA Finals.

Donovan said. "Never once has she questioned things — and that was the reputation she had. That she didn't like to share the ball, that she took too many shots. She's never been selfish here. There was no better fit for this team."

The Storm swept Minnesota in the first round of the 2004 WNBA play-offs, then eliminated the Sacramento Monarchs in the Western Conference finals to reach the WNBA Championships. Seattle faced the Connecticut Sun in a three-game series to decide the league championship. Lennox scored 17 points in Game 1, but the Storm lost to the Sun in Connecticut.

Facing possible elimination, the Storm returned to their home court for Game 2 of the WNBA Finals. In a close, hard-fought contest that came down to the final shot, Lennox turned in one of the best performances of her career. She led the Storm with 27 points on 11 for 16 shooting, which set a new playoff record for shooting accuracy at .636. The fourth quarter became a shooting duel between Lennox and Sun forward Nykesha Sales, as the two players exchanged baskets for several minutes. "Betty Lennox carried us," said Storm guard Sue Bird. "It was almost her vs. Nykesha at one point, going back and forth. I wouldn't be surprised if they scored all the points in the last three minutes. It was unbelievable to watch."

> "Betty Lennox carried us," said Storm guard Sue Bird about the WNBA Finals. "It was almost her vs. Nykesha at one point, going back and forth. I wouldn't be surprised if they scored all the points in the last three minutes. It was unbelievable to watch."

With the sellout crowd of 17,000 Storm fans chanting "Betty, Betty," Lennox lifted her team to victory and sent the finals into a deciding Game 3. "I just played my hardest, and playing in front of the fans here is very supportive," she said afterward. "I've never been part of an atmosphere that's so welcoming." Coach Donovan felt that the game was one of the most exciting the league had ever seen. "A great game for the WNBA, and for the state of this league," she declared. "Two players who weren't highlighted coming into this series took over, with one great play after the other from both ends. It was fun to watch."

Lennox continued to soar in Game 3, scoring a game-high 23 points to give the Storm a convincing 74-60 victory and its first WNBA title. When the final buzzer sounded, Lennox and her teammates piled on top of one another at center court as green-and-yellow confetti rained from the rafters. "It's an amazing feeling—I will cherish this forever," Lennox gushed afterward.

Lennox (22) holds the Most Valuable Player (MVP) trophy overhead as coach Anne Donovan (top) and teammates look on.

Lennox clearly elevated her game to a new level in the Finals. She averaged 22.3 points per game during the three-game series — double her season average — and shot an impressive 50 percent from the floor and a remarkable 60 percent from three-point range. She also added 4.3 rebounds and 2 assists per game. After the championship trophy was awarded, WNBA officials announced that Lennox had been named Most Valuable Player of the Finals. She felt overwhelmed by the award, which offered some redemption after an often-frustrating professional career. "Not only the celebration, the award that I just got — I can't believe it," she stated. "Me? After everything I've been through, and how many teams I've been on? I'm speechless."

Focusing on the Future

Lennox was a restricted free agent at the end of the 2004 campaign. This meant that she could entertain offers from other WNBA teams, but the Storm could retain her rights by matching any contracts she received. But Lennox expects to be back in Seattle for the 2005 season. In fact, after playing for so many different teams, she hopes to play out the rest of her career with the Storm. "My focus is to be part of the team and then be a franchise player and make it my home," she explained. "I'll feel more comfortable instead of hopping from team to team." Lennox also believes that the Storm can contend for the WNBA championship again in 2005. "This is a great young team that wants to be coached," Donovan stated. "They're not looking to settle for just one championship."

Over the course of her WNBA career, Lennox has averaged a solid 11.6 points, 4.1 rebounds, and 1.9 assists per game. She is known around the league for her work ethic, particularly in the weight room, where she can bench press a remarkable 165 pounds. "I think it helps me out a lot, because a lot of players don't like to lift," she noted. "Me, you have to get me out of the gym. I like it because it makes me feel good inside, makes me feel better on the court. I am small, but I play real big, have a big heart. In order to do all of that, first of all, you have to put in the dirty work, you have to put in the work in the weight room. That separates the good players from the great players." Whatever happens over the remaining years of her career, Lennox feels fortunate to have been able to earn a living playing the game she loves. "I just feel blessed that I'm living my dream and that I have the opportunity to do that," she said.

> *When WNBA officials announced that Lennox had been named Most Valuable Player of the Finals, she felt overwhelmed by the award. "Not only the celebration, the award that I just got—I can't believe it," she stated. "Me? After everything I've been through, and how many teams I've been on? I'm speechless."*

HOME AND FAMILY

Lennox, who is single, remains close to her family. Whenever she is away from home, she spends hours talking to her siblings on the telephone. She owns a home in Independence, Missouri, but lives in Seattle during the WNBA season.

HOBBIES AND OTHER INTERESTS

Lennox loves the Tasmanian Devil cartoon character and sports several tattoos with his likeness. "I'm a Taz fanatic," she acknowledged. "I like his speed and quickness. I kind of talk like him, too. I get carried away sometimes."

Lennox admits that she does not have an active social life. "My whole life outside of basketball is lifting weights and working out—by that time I'm

———— " ————

Lennox feels fortunate to have been able to earn a living playing the game she loves. "I just feel blessed that I'm living my dream and that I have the opportunity to do that," she said.

———— " ————

exhausted," she explained. "I don't go out, I don't hang around a lot of people. I'm not being selfish, that's just not my cup of tea."

Lennox does enjoy working in the community, however, especially with children. In fact, she was nominated for the WNBA's Community Assist Award in 2003. "I like being able to go out into the community and participate with kids, to touch them and be a positive role model," she stated. "Going out into the community and putting smiles on people's faces is what makes my day." Lennox hopes that her community service will prove useful in building a career as a youth counselor once her basketball days are over.

HONORS AND AWARDS

Junior College National Championship: 1996-1997, with Trinity Valley
    Community College
Sun Belt Conference Player of the Year: 1999-2000
All-American (U.S.A. Basketball Writers Association): 1999-2000
All-American (Women's Basketball News Service): 1999-2000
WNBA All-Star Team: 2000
WNBA Rookie of the Year: 2000
WNBA Championship: 2004, with the Seattle Storm
WNBA Finals Most Valuable Player: 2004

FURTHER READING

Books

Contemporary Black Biography, Vol. 31, 2001

Periodicals

Houston Chronicle, Oct. 13, 2004, Sports, p.13
Kansas City Star, May 25, 1995, p.D7; Mar. 26, 1999, p.D6; Aug. 2, 2000,
    p.D1; Feb. 16, 2001, p.D1; Oct. 12, 2004, p.C3
Minneapolis Star-Tribune, July 7, 2000, p.C1; Aug. 11, 2000, p.C1; Aug. 12,
    2000, p.C4; June 12, 2002, p.C1; July 19, 2002, p.C6

Palm Beach (FL) Post, July 19, 2002, p.B2
Seattle Post-Intelligencer, July 21, 2004, p.D1; Oct. 11, 2004, p.D1
Seattle Times, June 21, 2004, p.C4; July 12, 2004, p.C10
Sports Illustrated, Feb. 7, 2000, p.74; Oct. 25, 2004, p.8
Tacoma (WA) News Tribune, Oct. 11, 2004, p.C5; Oct. 13, 2004, p.C1

Online Articles

http://seattletimes.nwsource.com
   (*Seattle Times,* "Who Is Betty Lennox?" Oct. 12, 2004)
http://www.wnba.com/storm/news
   (WNBA.com, "Lennox Looking for a Home" and "Lennox's Butterfly
   Effect," 2004)

Online Databases

Biography Resource Center Online, 2005, article from *Contemporary Black
Biography,* 2001

ADDRESS

Betty Lennox
Seattle Storm
351 Elliott Avenue West
Suite 500
Seattle, WA 98119

WORLD WIDE WEB SITE

http://www.wnba.com

Michael Phelps 1985-

American Swimmer
Winner of Six Gold Medals at the 2004 Olympic
Games

BIRTH

Michael Fred Phelps was born on June 30, 1985, in Baltimore,
Maryland. His father, Fred Phelps, is a retired Maryland State
Police officer. His mother, Debbie Phelps, is a former Maryland
teacher of the year who later became a Baltimore County
school administrator. Michael's parents divorced when he was
nine years old. He and his two older sisters, Hilary and Whitney, were raised primarily by their mother.

YOUTH

Michael Phelps has been involved in swimming almost from the time he was born. His older sisters started taking swimming lessons when he was a toddler, and his mother brought him along to all of their practices and meets. "I remember taking him out of his crib, putting him in the car, and driving to practice or a competition," Debbie Phelps recalled. "He grew up around the pool." Before long, Michael decided to try the sport himself. He overcame an early fear of putting his face in the water to join the North Baltimore Aquatic Club (NBAC) at the age of seven.

The NBAC is one of the premier competitive swimming clubs in the United States. Over the years it has produced a dozen Olympians. All three of the Phelps children proved to be talented swimmers, especially Michael's sister Whitney. Ranked third in the world by the time she was 15, Whitney appeared likely to make the U.S. Olympic Team that would compete in the 1996 Games in Atlanta, Georgia. Unfortunately, Whitney suffered a back injury that prevented her from qualifying for the Olympics and eventually forced her to quit the sport. "That devastated us," Michael recalled years later. "She was extremely talented. With the times she swam, she would still be a player today."

> **"**
>
> *"Michael was a goofy little kid, but when it came to a swim meet, he wanted to win," said his first coach, Tom Himes. "He was just like any other little kid. When he got tired, little things became big issues. He would throw his goggles and have a fit in practice, which was always a challenge for him. When I'd get on him about doing something that he wasn't doing in the right way, his defense was tears."*
>
> **"**

Michael possessed a strong competitive drive from the start of his swimming career, but his immaturity sometimes showed. "Michael was a goofy little kid, but when it came to a swim meet, he wanted to win," said his first coach, Tom Himes. "He was just like any other little kid. When he got tired, little things became big issues. He would throw his goggles and have a fit in practice, which was always a challenge for him. When I'd get on him about doing something that he wasn't doing in the right way, his defense was tears."

When Michael was 11 years old, he began training with a new coach, Bob Bowman. A short time later, Bowman pulled Debbie Phelps aside and told her that Michael was an extraordinarily gifted swimmer who had the potential to make it to the Olympics someday. "I'm thinking, this man is crazy," she remembered. "This is my 11-year-old baby." Bowman's confidence inspired Michael to quit playing other sports and focus all of his attention on swimming. "He told me, 'If you want to focus on something, you could be in the Olympics,'" Michael related. "When I heard that, I perked my ears up. Everyone, I think, as a little kid wants to do something big, like be in the Olympics. Everyone wants to be the best—an American icon."

> "
>
> Bowman's confidence inspired Phelps to quit playing other sports and focus all of his attention on swimming. "He told me, 'If you want to focus on something, you could be in the Olympics,'" Phelps related. "When I heard that, I perked my ears up. Everyone, I think, as a little kid wants to do something big, like be in the Olympics. Everyone wants to be the best—an American icon."
>
> "

From that time on, Phelps practiced swimming twice a day—for a total of about five hours—six days per week. Still, his mother insisted that he did not miss out on leading a normal life as a teenager. "There was always a balance," she said. "He went to basketball games. He went to football games. He had friends. He was a normal kid. But he always came home early and got his sleep and went to practice the next day."

Unlike most competitive swimmers—who tend to specialize in a particular stroke and distance—Phelps showed promise in 100-meter sprints as well as 400-meter endurance races. He was also highly competitive in all four strokes: freestyle, backstroke, breaststroke, and butterfly. As a result, Bowman decided to base Phelps's training around the individual medley (IM), an event in which competitors swim each of the four strokes for one leg of the race. "All the events complement each other, so working on all of them makes sense," the coach explained. The two individual medley events are the 200-meter IM, in which competitors use each stroke for 50 meters, and the 400-meter IM, in which swimmers use each stroke for 100 meters. There are also medley relay events involving teams of four swimmers, such as the 4 x 100 medley relay. In these events, each member of the team completes one leg of the race using a different stroke.

Phelps with his longtime coach, Bob Bowman.

EDUCATION

Throughout his school years, Phelps always had trouble sitting still and paying attention in class. "He was a very energetic boy who drove all his teachers crazy," his mother noted. He was diagnosed with attention deficit disorder (ADD) in elementary school and took medication to help him focus for several years. But the condition improved once he began intensive swim practices at the age of 11.

Phelps attended Towson High School in Towson, Maryland. By that point, he was already a nationally ranked competitive swimmer. In fact, he missed the start of his sophomore year in order to compete at the 2000 Olympic Games in Sydney, Australia. Upon his return, he was greeted by 1,200 fellow students cheering on the front lawn of the school. Before the start of his junior year in 2001, Phelps had broken his first world record and signed an endorsement contract with Speedo that made him a professional athlete. After graduating from high school in 2003, he took a year off in order to train for the 2004 Olympic Games in Athens, Greece.

In January 2005 Phelps enrolled as a student at the University of Michigan in Ann Arbor, where Bowman had accepted a job as coach of the swim team. Phelps planned to major in sports management. "School is important because it will give him a normal experience that other people his age are getting," Bowman explained. "He really doesn't have a lot of normal experiences anymore." As a professional, Phelps was not eligible to compete in college swimming events. But he served as an assistant for the university team and also trained with Club Wolverine, a world-class swimming club that included many Michigan swimmers as well as college graduates and professionals.

―――― " ――――

At the 2000 Olympics, Phelps felt nervous and distracted. "I was just a mess. The environment controlled me," he recalled. "People were saying [fifth] was good, and I was saying, 'No, it's not. I want more.' It's something that's been with me ever since."

―――― " ――――

CAREER HIGHLIGHTS

Setting Early Records

Phelps began his swimming career at a young age. In fact, he showed so much promise as a young swimmer that he made the USA Swimming B Team at the age of 14, in 1999. Between the spring of 1999 and the summer of 2000, Phelps grew a remarkable eight inches and added 60 pounds to his lean frame. The growth spurt only made him faster in the water.

In 2000, before starting his sophomore year in high school, Phelps made the USA Swimming A Team and competed in the U.S. Olympic Trials. The top two swimmers in each event would qualifiy for the team that would represent the United States at the 2000 Games in Sydney, Australia. Phelps finished second in the 200-meter butterfly event and qualified for the U.S. Olympic Team. At age 15, he was the youngest male athlete in more than 60 years to qualify for the U.S. Olympic Team.

At the Sydney Games, Phelps performed well enough in his preliminary heat to make the final field for the 200 butterfly. As his race approached, however, he felt nervous and distracted. "I was just a mess," he recalled. "The environment controlled me." The high school sophomore finished a respectable fifth, missing the bronze medal by just three-tenths of a second and breaking an American record for his age group. Nevertheless, Phelps expressed disappointment with his performance. "People were saying [fifth] was good, and I was saying, 'No, it's not. I want more,'" he noted. "It's something that's been with me ever since."

In 2001 Phelps became the youngest male athlete in history to set a world record by swimming the 200-meter butterfly in 1 minute, 54.92 seconds at the U.S. Spring National Championships. "When I hit the wall, I turned around and saw the scoreboard flashing 'New World Record,'" he remembered. "I especially remember Tom [Malchow] congratulating me. That meant a lot, since he's an excellent swimmer, a great competitor, and the one who had held the world record. Then I remember I jumped out of the water and went nuts. I don't think I've ever smiled so big before."

Phelps continued his string of impressive performances at the 2001 World Championships in Japan. At a meet dominated by Ian Thorpe of Australia, who won six gold medals, Phelps broke his own world record in the 200 fly with a time of 1:54.58 to claim his first world title. "It felt awesome," he said afterward. "This is the first medal I've ever won in an international meet. For it to be gold is incredible. It feels great. I can't explain it." USA Swimming recognized Phelps's achievements by naming him Swimmer of the Year for 2001.

Following his outstanding 2001 season, Phelps signed an endorsement contract with Speedo that made him one of the youngest male athletes ever to turn professional. The deal provided income to pay for his training and his travel expenses. But becoming a professional meant that he gave up his eligibility to compete in collegiate swimming.

Emerging as a Dominant Force

Over the next two seasons, Phelps emerged as one of the most dominant male swimmers in the world. At the 2002 U.S. Summer National Championships he won four events—the 200-meter butterfly, the 100-meter butterfly, the 200-meter IM, and the 400-meter IM. His time of 4:11.09 in the 400 IM set a new world record. The following year he won national titles in three different strokes at the 2003 U.S. Spring National Championships, swimming to victory in the 200-meter freestyle, the 200-meter backstroke, and the 100-meter butterfly.

Phelps first gained international stardom at the 2003 World Championships in Barcelona, Spain. He became the first swimmer ever to set five individual world records in a single meet, including two in one day. He lowered his own record in the 200 fly to 1:53.93, and he also set records in winning the 200 IM and 400 IM. For Phelps, though, the defining moment of the meet came when he set a personal best time of 51.10 seconds in the 100-meter butterfly, only to be defeated in a world-record performance by his U.S. teammate Ian Crocker. The loss bothered Phelps so much that he

Three different views of Phelps doing the butterfly.

put a picture of Crocker on his bedroom wall to inspire him to train harder. It was one of only two losses that Phelps suffered all year.

At the 2003 U.S. Summer National Championships Phelps became the first man ever to win five national titles at a single meet. His achievements included setting a new world record in the 200 IM with a time of 1:55.94—more than two seconds faster than anyone else had ever swum the event. He was particularly excited by this record, because it meant that Bowman had to follow through on a promise to shave his head if his star swimmer broke 1:56 in the event. Phelps also won the 100-meter freestyle, an event that he entered on a whim to see if he could go fast enough to qualify for the U.S. 4 x 100-meter freestyle relay team (in which four different swimmers each complete a 100-meter freestyle in succession). An hour later, he turned in the third-fastest time in history in the 200-meter backstroke. His extraordinary success in 2003 earned him a second Swimmer of the Year Award, as well as the prestigious James E. Sullivan Award as the nation's top amateur athlete.

"I love to race the best people in the world and the fastest people in the world," Phelps once said. "It definitely makes things fun and keeps things interesting."

Qualifying for the Olympics

At the 2004 U.S. National Championships Phelps repeated his feat of winning five national titles. Perhaps the most notable events of the meet were the 100-meter and 200-meter backstroke, both of which he lost to backstroke specialist Aaron Peirsol. "I love to race the best people in the world and the fastest people in the world," Phelps said afterward. "It definitely makes things fun and keeps things interesting."

The next major event in American swimming was the U.S. Olympic Trials, where the nation's top swimmers competed for spots on the team that would represent the United States at the 2004 Olympic Games in Athens, Greece. Phelps turned in a phenomenal performance at the trials, becoming the first American swimmer ever to qualify to compete in six individual events at the Olympics. He won the 200-meter butterfly and both the 200 and 400 IM, setting a new world record in the latter event. He also qualified for the 200-meter backstroke by finishing second to Peirsol, and for the 100-meter butterfly by finishing second to Ian Crocker. Both competitors set world records in defeating Phelps. "Nothing I do over there [in

Athens] will be easy," he said afterward. "I knew that before I got into this. Off of this performance we can change some things and work on some things."

The final event in which Phelps qualified for the Olympics was the 200-meter freestyle. Although it was not his strongest event, he decided to try it in hopes of competing head-to-head against Australia's Ian Thorpe, who had won three gold medals and two silver medals at the 2000 Games. "One thing I always wanted to do was race Thorpe in a freestyle event," Phelps explained. "I think it is the best opportunity for me to be able to swim in probably the fastest 200 freestyle heat in history." "We've always used Ian a little bit as a yardstick," Bowman added. "Having someone like that who really is light years ahead of everyone else is tremendously motivational. If Michael were the only one, I think it would be hard to keep pushing him." Finally, Phelps's strong performance at the U.S. Olympic Trials also earned him a spot on at least two American relay teams—the 4 x 200 freestyle relay and the 4 x 100 medley relay.

> "That was one of the most exciting moments I've had in sports. Something I'll never forget," Phelps said after Mark Spitz joined Phelps on the podium at the Olympic Trials. "One of the things he said was that he's behind me, and he knows what I'm going through. He told me to focus on swimming. He's going to be there in Athens, cheering me on. To have one of the best of all time shake your hand and hold it up, say he's behind you 100 percent, that's motivation."

Chasing Mark Spitz's Record

When Phelps qualified to compete in eight Olympic events—including six individual events and two relays—many observers felt that he might have a chance to break the all-time record of seven gold medals that had been set by American swimmer Mark Spitz at the 1972 Games in Munich, Germany. Spitz collected his medals by winning four individual events and contributing to three relay victories. In those days, the American men were dominant in relay events, and their margins of victory in the three gold medal races ranged from three to six seconds. Counting preliminary heats, Spitz swam a total of 13 races in the Olympic Games.

Phelps faced a much more difficult challenge in attempting to match Spitz's record of seven gold medals. Preliminary heats had been added in several events since 1972, so Phelps would have to compete at least 17 times over eight days—sometimes more than once in an hour—in order to have a chance at winning seven gold medals. In addition, international competition had become so fierce by 2004 that most swimmers specialized in a single stroke and distance. In the individual events, therefore, Phelps would face the world's best swimmers, most of whom had dedicated their training to that one event. Finally, the American relay teams were not as strong as they were in Spitz's day, further reducing the odds that Phelps could collect seven golds. In fact, the American men were only favored to win one relay event, the 4 x 100 medley relay.

Phelps with Mark Spitz, former Olympic swimmer and seven-time Olympic gold medal winner, on the podium at the U.S. Olympic Trials.

At the awards ceremony following the Olympic Trials, Mark Spitz appeared to present one of Phelps's medals. Encouraged by 10,000 cheering fans, Spitz joined Phelps on the podium, raised his hand in the air, and gave him some words of encouragement for the upcoming Games. "That was one of the most exciting moments I've had in sports. Something I'll never forget," Phelps said afterward. "One of the things he said was that he's behind me, and he knows what I'm going through. He told me to focus on swimming. He's going to be there in Athens, cheering me on. To have one of the best of all time shake your hand and hold it up, say he's behind you 100 percent, that's motivation." Adding to the motivation, Speedo announced that it would pay Phelps a $1 million bonus if he succeeded in breaking Spitz's record.

As the Athens Games approached, many experts speculated that scheduling conflicts would force Phelps to drop one of the six individual events for which he had qualified. He remained secretive about his plans for several weeks. Although some of his rivals expressed annoyance at his refusal to reveal his plans, Phelps seemed to enjoy keeping them guessing. "Why do they have to know?" he asked. "Wouldn't it be better for them just to concentrate on their own events and not worry about what I'm doing?"

Finally, a few weeks before the Olympics began, Phelps announced that he was withdrawing from the 200-meter backstroke competition. His decision surprised many people, because he was virtually guaranteed to win at least a silver medal in that event. Instead, he decided to compete in one of his weaker events, the 200-meter freestyle, in order to face Ian Thorpe. "If this was just about seven gold medals, he would have dropped this event," Bowman said of the 200 free. "But that's not the goal. The goal is to see what he can do." Phelps also tried to downplay the significance of chasing Spitz's record. "My goal is to win one Olympic medal," he stated. "One will not be a failure to me."

Winning Six Gold Medals

Once the Olympic Games got underway, Phelps more than met the high expectations that had preceded his trip to Athens. He won gold medals in his three best individual events—the 200 butterfly (with a time of 1:54.04), the 200 IM (with a time of 1:57.14), and the 400 IM (with a world record time of 4:09.09). He earned a fourth individual gold in the 100 butterfly, overcoming a slow start to beat teammate Ian Crocker by .04 seconds. He thus tied Spitz's record of four individual swimming gold medals in a single Olympics.

Phelps's final individual event, the 200 freestyle, featured one of the strongest fields in the history of competitive swimming. In addition to Phelps and favorite Ian Thorpe, the "race of the century" included defending Olympic champion Pieter van den Hoogenband of the Netherlands, Grant Hackett of Australia, and Klete Keller of the United States. Van den Hoogenband took an early lead, but Thorpe charged past him in the final 50 meters to claim the gold with a time of 1:44.71. Phelps nearly caught the Dutchman as well, but he ended up settling for the bronze—despite setting a new American record of 1:45.32. "I was happy to be part of this field and to do my best time," he said afterward. "It was fun."

Halfway through the Olympic swimming competition, USA Swimming coaches announced that they were adding Phelps to the American 4 x 100 freestyle relay team. Some of his teammates were upset by the decision. Since Phelps had not qualified for the event at the Olympic Trials, they wondered if the coaches were adding him at the last minute in order to improve his chances of winning seven gold medals. Despite the presence

*Phelps (center) celebrating with teammates after winning the gold medal in the
4 x 200 meter freestyle relay.*

of Phelps, though, the American men had to settle for bronze in the event
behind South Africa and the Netherlands. Phelps's teammate Ian Crocker,
who had been complaining of a sore throat, swam a disastrously slow first
leg that left the other three American swimmers struggling to catch up.

Phelps's favorite race of the Athens Games was the 4 x 200 freestyle relay. The American men — once dominant in the event — had not won it in international competition in seven years, and Phelps and his teammates were determined to restore the U.S. to glory. Competing just one hour after winning gold in the 200 fly, Phelps swam a blistering leadoff leg that gave the American team a body-length lead. He then climbed out of the water and watched intently while his teammates completed their legs. When American anchor Klete Keller held off a charging Ian Thorpe and touched the wall first, Phelps raised his arms and whooped with joy. "That was the most exciting race I have ever been a part of," he said afterward. "I don't think I have ever celebrated like that in my life." His medal total stood at seven, with five gold and two bronze.

Phelps's final race of the 2004 Olympics was the 4 x 100 medley relay, in which he was scheduled to swim the butterfly leg. By this time, though, he was feeling the effects of the strenuous eight-day competition. He also knew that, since he had competed in the preliminary heat of the event, he would share any medal that the U.S. team earned. In what USA Swimming Coach Eddie Reese called "a hell of a gesture," Phelps decided to give up his spot on the relay team. The night before the race, he offered his spot to teammate Ian Crocker, who had yet to win a gold medal. In fact, Crocker had cost Phelps a chance at winning seven golds with his poor performance in the 4 x 100 freestyle relay. "Ian's one of the greatest relay swimmers in history," Phelps noted. "I was willing to give him another chance." Crocker found his teammate's generosity hard to believe. "I'm speechless," he said. "It's a huge gift, but difficult to accept. It makes me want to just go out there and tear up the pool tomorrow."

> —— " ——
>
> *Phelps's favorite race of the Athens Games was the 4 x 200 freestyle relay. When American anchor Klete Keller held off a charging Ian Thorpe and touched the wall first, Phelps raised his arms and whooped with joy. "That was the most exciting race I have ever been a part of," he said afterward. "I don't think I have ever celebrated like that in my life."*
>
> —— " ——

On the final day of the Olympic swimming competition, Phelps watched from the stands as his teammates won the 4 x 100 medley relay with a world record time of 3:30.68. He thus earned his sixth gold medal of the Athens Games, falling one short of matching Spitz's record. Counting his two bronze medals, though, his total of eight tied the all-time record for an individual competitor in a single games, and was the most ever in a non-boycotted Olympiad. (The only other person to win eight medals was a Russian gymnast who achieved the feat in 1980, when the United States and several European countries did not compete due to political disputes.)

Phelps's coaches and teammates were quick to praise his accomplishments, despite the fact that he had not managed to break Spitz's record. "To try to make the story that he's a failure—he's not," said American backstroker Aaron Peirsol. "He's the greatest swimmer in the world right now. He's incredible, unbelievable. What he's done is really spectacular in this day and age. To come away with eight medals, that really is the Spitzian accomplishment of our age." Many in-

"There's nobody in the last 20 years, in any sport, who can say they did what Michael did this week," said USA Swimming Coach Eddie Reese. "He was born to swim, and he has great talent, great versatility, and great resiliency. And he does the hardest workouts in the world. You can't beat that combination until he retires."

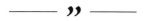

siders pointed out that, in addition to competitions, the demands facing Phelps at the Games included mandatory drug tests, medal ceremonies, team meetings, and nonstop interviews. He somehow managed to remain calm, healthy, and good natured despite all the pressure. "There's nobody in the last 20 years, in any sport, who can say they did what Michael did this week," Reese added. "He was born to swim, and he has great talent, great versatility, and great resiliency. And he does the hardest workouts in the world. You can't beat that combination until he retires."

Struggling to Regain His Form

A few months after the Olympics, Phelps was forced to withdraw from the 2004 Short-Course World Championships due to a back injury. The injury concerned him because it was similar to the one that had prematurely ended his sister Whitney's swimming career. In addition, he had spent so much time in the water training for Athens that he felt out of sorts when he could not swim. "When I'm not swimming, I have no idea what to do with myself," he admitted. "Nothing to look forward to, no goals, nothing. Just killing time. Just hanging on."

Phelps shows his form on the starting blocks.

In November 2004 Phelps attended a party with some friends. Since he did not have an early morning practice session the next day, he stayed late and drank alcohol. But then he made the decision to drive. On his way home, he ran a stop sign, was pulled over by the police, and was arrested for driving under the influence of alcohol (DUI). Phelps immediately admitted his mistake and apologized for it. He also spoke out publicly about the dangers of drinking and driving, and answered questions about his own experience and the effect it had on him and his family. "I've made a mistake and it's something I'm going to have to live with now," he noted.

"I want to reach out as much as I can to help as many kids as I can to get the message not to drink and drive. It's unacceptable and just flat-out wrong. It's a big learning experience, and I want to move forward from here. The hardest thing is knowing the people I have let down." In December Phelps pleaded guilty to DUI. The judge considered his long record of community service in handing down a sentence of 18 months probation, after which his record will be wiped clean.

In 2005 Phelps moved to Ann Arbor, Michigan, and enrolled as a student at the University of Michigan. He also published his autobiography, *Michael Phelps: Beneath the Surface*. Once his back injury healed, he resumed training with Bowman at Club Wolverine in preparation for the 2005 World Championships. Many experts predict that Phelps could remain one of the world's top swimmers for another ten years. After all, he will only be 27 years old at the time of the 2012 Olympic Games. "Michael is the most talented swimmer in the world," said Reese. "The tough part for everyone else is he's also the hardest-working. It's a rare phenomenon. You never see it." "He's a dream in the water, mesmerizing to watch," added Olympic swimmer Debbie Meyer. "You think of a porpoise. You wonder how a human being can do that."

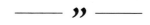

"What Michael knows how to do, everybody else had to learn," said his NBAC teammate Kevin Clements. "And most of it, he knew the first time he got in the water."

Some people attribute Phelps's extraordinary skills to genetics. His natural advantages include a long torso and exceptionally long arms, but short legs. "With that arm length, he has a much greater range of motion with his stroke," Bowman explained. "His legs are not particularly long, and that helps him ride high in the water." Phelps also possesses hyperflexible joints that give him more freedom of movement than most of his competitors, and size 14 feet that act like big flippers to propel him through the water. He also has a freakish ability to recover quickly after races because his body produces less lactate—the substance that makes muscles feel tired after exertion—than most athletes. This allows him to race more frequently than his competitors. Finally, Phelps has a natural "feel" for the water that is the envy of many other swimmers. "What Michael knows how to do, everybody else had to learn," said his NBAC teammate Kevin Clements. "And most of it, he knew the first time he got in the water." His only weakness is that he has relatively slow reaction time, which often makes him the last competitor to leave the starting blocks.

> "I remember looking up to a bunch of swimmers—I still do," Phelps said. "It wasn't long ago that I was that young boy or girl, wanting to be just like the swimmers I looked up to. I just try to be myself, and act normal. What they see is what they get with me. I'm so glad because I can really relate to them."

In addition to his outstanding abilities in the pool, Phelps has become a fan favorite for his good humor and willingness to spend time with young swimmers and sign autographs. "I remember looking up to a bunch of swimmers—I still do," he said. "It wasn't long ago that I was that young boy or girl, wanting to be just like the swimmers I looked up to. I just try to be myself, and act normal. What they see is what they get with me. I'm so glad because I can really relate to them." Phelps claims that his ultimate goal is to help swimming become more than a sport that enters the public consciousness every four years during the Olympics. "We need to get swimming in the headlines. We need to be on 'SportsCenter,'" he noted. "I want to do anything I can to help the sport grow. One of my big goals is to change the fact that swimmers don't get much attention. . . . I can't stress enough how important that is to me."

HOME AND FAMILY

Phelps, who is single, purchased a home in 2005 in Ann Arbor, Michigan.

HOBBIES AND OTHER INTERESTS

In his free time, Phelps enjoys listening to rap music by such artists as Eminem and DMX, watching movie comedies starring Adam Sandler and Chris Farley, and playing video games. He is also active in several charitable causes. For example, he serves as the national spokesman for Boys and Girls Clubs of America, is an honorary board member of Pathfinders for Autism, and has volunteered at the Child Life Center at Johns Hopkins University.

WRITINGS

Michael Phelps: Beneath the Surface, 2005 (with Brian Cazeneuve)

HONORS AND AWARDS

Swimmer of the Year (USA Swimming): 2001, 2003
James E. Sullivan Award (Amateur Athletic Union): 2003
Olympic Swimming, 100-meter butterfly: 2004, gold medal
Olympic Swimming, 200-meter butterfly: 2004, gold medal
Olympic Swimming, 200-meter individual medley: 2004, gold medal
Olympic Swimming, 400-meter individual medley: 2004, gold medal
Olympic Swimming, 4 x 100-meter medley relay: 2004, gold medal
Olympic Swimming, 4 x 200-meter freestyle relay: 2004, gold medal
Olympic Swimming, 200-meter freestyle: 2004, bronze medal
Olympic Swimming, 4 x 100-meter freestyle relay: 2004, bronze medal
Athlete of the Year (*Sports Illustrated for Kids*): 2004
World Swimmer of the Year (*Swimming World*): 2004

FURTHER READING

Books

Phelps, Michael, with Brian Cazeneuve. *Michael Phelps: Beneath the Surface,*
   2005
Who's Who in America, 2005

Periodicals

Baltimore Sun, Aug. 13, 2000, p.A1; Jan. 14, 2001, p.F9; July 25, 2001, p.A1;
   July 11, 2004, p.E1; Aug. 8, 2004, p.A1; Nov. 14, 2004, p.B1; Dec. 30, 2004,
   p.B1
Boys' Life, Aug. 2004, p.14
Chicago Tribune, July 4, 2004, Sports, p.1
Current Biography Yearbook, 2004
Detroit Free Press, Dec. 18, 2004, p.B1
ESPN Magazine, Apr. 11, 2005, p.106
New York Times Magazine, Aug. 8, 2004, p.22
Newsweek, Aug. 16, 2004, p.40; Aug. 30, 2004, p.16
Sports Illustrated, Aug. 6, 2001, p.74; Aug. 23, 2004, p.46; Aug. 30, 2004,
   p.58
Sports Illustrated for Kids, Aug. 2004, p.26; Jan. 2005, p.38
Swimming World, June 2001, p.27; Dec. 2004, p.16; Sep. 2003, p.30;
   Oct. 2003, p.22; Sep. 2004, p.18
USA Today, Aug. 14, 2000, p.C3; Aug. 13, 2002, p.C10; July 7, 2004, p.C1;
   July 14, 2004, p.C3; Aug. 13, 2004, p.F4

Online Articles

http://www.si.com
   (*Sports Illustrated,* "My Sportsman Choice: Michael Phelps," Nov. 26, 2004)

Online Databases

Biography Resource Center Online, 2005

ADDRESS

Michael Phelps
USA Swimming
1 Olympic Plaza
Colorado Springs, CO 80809

WORLD WIDE WEB SITES

http://www.michaelphelps.com
http://www.usaswimming.org
http://www.usolympicteam.com
http://www.fina.org

Manny Ramirez 1972-

Dominican-Born American Baseball Player with the
Boston Red Sox
Most Valuable Player of the 2004 World Series

BIRTH

Manuel Aristides Ramirez, known by the nickname Manny,
was born on May 30, 1972, in Santo Domingo, Dominican
Republic. Manny was the only son among five children born
to Aristides and Onelcidad Ramirez.

Manny spent his early years in the Dominican Republic, near
Cuba in the Caribbean Sea. The Dominican Republic and Haiti

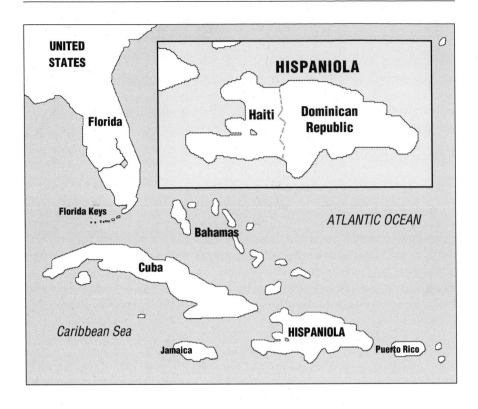

together make up the island of Hispaniola, which is part of the chain of islands known as the West Indies. Much of the region is quite poor. Manny's parents hoped to provide their children with greater opportunities in life, so they moved to the United States in 1983. They settled in the Washington Heights neighborhood of New York City, which was a popular destination for newly arrived Dominican immigrants. Aristides found work as a cab driver, while Onelcidad became a seamstress in a garment factory. Manny and his sisters joined their parents in New York City in 1985, and Manny became an American citizen in 2004.

YOUTH

Baseball is the most popular sport in the Dominican Republic. Many skilled Dominican players have left the economically depressed nation to play Major League Baseball in the United States, and their success has inspired countless young Dominican boys to take up the game. As a result, baseball was a big part of Ramirez's life from a very early age. His grandmother helped ignite his love for the sport by bringing him a baseball glove and a child-sized Los Angeles Dodgers uniform after a visit to the United States.

Ramirez started playing baseball at the age of six, and it did not take long for him to develop an obsession with the game. "Since early on, the qualities that stood out were his firm determination and his desire to play baseball," his father remembered. "When he was six or seven, on many occasions his lunch and dinner had to be taken to the baseball field where he was playing.""My mom would get upset,"Manny acknowledged, "because I never came home in time to eat at the table with the rest of the family. I was always at the field playing."

In his early youth in the Dominican Republic, Ramirez's life followed a comfortable routine. He played baseball every morning, took a necessary break for school, and then returned to the field every afternoon and played until the sun went down. But his lifestyle underwent a significant disruption when he moved to the United States at age 13. Ramirez suddenly found himself in a strange country with no friends, and he faced such dangers as gangs, guns, and drug dealers in his Washington Heights neighborhood.

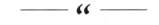

"All my friends and I were so into baseball, it probably kept us out of trouble," Ramirez recalled.

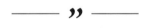

Once Ramirez discovered the local baseball diamonds, though, he started to feel at home. He made many new friends who shared two common goals — playing baseball whenever possible, and staying away from gangs and drugs. "All my friends and I were so into baseball, it probably kept us out of trouble,"he recalled. Although Ramirez loved playing baseball, it took a while for him to develop his natural talents. In fact, the teenager struggled during his early Little League days. "I was the ninth batter,"he recalled. "Everybody used to laugh at me."

Through hard work and determination, though, Ramirez became the best ballplayer in his neighborhood within a year of his arrival in New York. He showed particular promise at the plate. Whenever he came up to bat during a game, the opposing players would yell for their outfielders to move back *"a lapiscina, a lapiscina"* ("to the swimming pool, to the swimming pool"), because Ramirez often hit the ball over the swimming pool that was located in the far reaches of the outfield.

EDUCATION

Upon entering George Washington High School at the age of 15, Ramirez immediately became the star of the baseball team. He found that the baseball field was the one place he felt at home during his high school years. "In high school, I passed my classes but I never felt relaxed in class," he remembered. "I had just come to New York, to a different culture, and I was trying to fit in. Also, I was trying to learn a different language. I always like to do things correctly, and it was difficult learning correct English, so I lost interest. That got me even deeper into baseball. When I played, I felt good about myself, because I could do my best. I could work hard and help our team to win."

During his high school years, Ramirez became known throughout the neighborhood for his workout regimen. He woke up at 4:30 every morning to lift weights, and he often carried a car tire on his back for 20 blocks to increase his leg strength. He never missed a day of baseball practice, and he often stayed after practice to work on his skills and talk baseball with his coach, Steve Mandl.

All that hard work paid off. Ramirez batted .630 as a high school player and hit a home run in every 5.7 at bats. He was known far and wide for the distance his home runs traveled. As a senior, he hit two home runs in one game against Brandeis High that both flew over 430 feet. He was named to the all-city baseball team three times, and in his senior year he was named the New York City Public School Player of the Year. During his four years at George Washington High, his team won three Manhattan division championships.

> "Manny's a legend around here," said Coach Mandl from George Washington High. "I can talk to my kids all about goals, and they can make it by hard work, but unless they see it firsthand, it doesn't have the same impact. But Manny's something tangible. They all know him. Know what he had to do to get where he is. He's something for them to grasp. He's one of them."

Although Ramirez fell just short of graduating with his class in 1991, he later passed the high-school equivalency exam to earn his diploma. His success continues to inspire students at George Washington High. "Manny's a legend around here," Coach Mandl noted. "I can talk to my kids all about goals, and they can make it by hard work, but unless they see it firsthand, it doesn't have the same impact. But Manny's something tangible. They all know him. Know what he had to do to get where he is. He's something for them to grasp. He's one of them."

CAREER HIGHLIGHTS

Playing in the Minor Leagues

Ramirez's performance on the baseball field at George Washington High —as well as in summer leagues and in the Connie Mack World Series in 1989 and 1990—brought him to the attention of big-league scouts. In June 1991 he became the 13th player selected in the first round of the Major League Baseball draft by the Cleveland Indians. "I have never seen a high school player who can swing a bat like that," explained Indians' scout Joe DeLucca. "We think he's probably the best hitter in the draft. And he's a nice kid."

"I have never seen a high school player who can swing a bat like that," explained Cleveland Indians' scout Joe DeLucca. "We think he's probably the best hitter in the draft. And he's a nice kid."

Ramirez was thrilled to be rewarded for all his hard work. "It's like a dream," he said. "After I got drafted and got to my home, I said to my mother, 'You're not going to work anymore, Mom.'" After signing a contract, he was assigned to the Indians' Class A minor-league team in Burlington, North Carolina. In baseball, many players start playing for a team in the minor leagues, also called the farm system. The teams in the minor leagues are affiliated with those in the major leagues. There are a variety of minor leagues, which are ranked according to the level of competition. The top or best league is Class AAA (called Triple A), next is Class AA, then Class A, then below that are the rookie leagues. Players hope to move up through the system to a Class AAA team and then to the major leagues. Indeed, this was exactly the route that Ramirez took, starting out in Class A and moving up to Double- and Triple-A before reaching the majors.

Playing for the Indians' minor-league team, Ramirez struggled at first, both on and off the field. After one particularly rough game in which he had no hits in four at-bats, he became so discouraged that he thought about quitting. "I can't play," he told his roommate. "I can't hit. I'm going home." But Ramirez decided to stick it out, and before long he regained his form and began terrorizing opposing pitchers. He ended up hitting .329 in his first minor-league season and led the Appalachian League with 146 total bases, 19 home runs, 65 runs batted in (RBIs), and a .679 slugging percentage. The league's managers named him the Appalachian League Most Valuable Player, and *Baseball America* named him its Short-Season Player of the Year (lower-level minor-league teams play two short seasons each summer instead of one long season).

In 1992 Ramirez was transferred to the Indians' Class A affiliate in Kinston, North Carolina. A hand injury limited him to only 81 games that season, but his hitting skills continued to develop. Although he faced better pitching in the Carolina League, he hit .278 with 18 doubles, 12 home runs, and 63 RBIs. At the end of the season, he was named the league's "most exciting player."

Ramirez started the 1993 season at the Double-A level, playing for Canton-Akron in Ohio. After posting an impressive .340 average over the first half of the season, he earned a promotion in July to the Indians' Triple-A team in Charlotte, North Carolina. In 129 games split between Canton-Akron and Charlotte, Ramirez ended up hitting .333 with 31 home runs and 115 RBIs. *Baseball America* recognized Ramirez as its Minor League Player of the Year and rated him as the second-best prospect in the Eastern League.

> *Ramirez made his major-league debut at historic Yankee Stadium, where the Indians were playing the New York Yankees. Playing in front of 50 friends and family members, he went 3-for-4 in that game, hitting a double and two home runs. "It was unbelievable," he said later. "I remember I felt so funny in [my stomach], like the butterfly."*

Reaching the Major Leagues — the Cleveland Indians

Ramirez's stunning performance in the minor leagues served notice to the Indians that he was ready to play in the majors. On September 1, 1993 — the day that big league teams were allowed to expand their rosters to bring up more young players for the playoffs — he received a call to join the Cleveland Indians. Ramirez did not know it at that time, but he would never play another day in the minor leagues.

Ramirez made his major-league debut in storybook fashion by starting a game at historic Yankee Stadium, where the Indians were playing the New York Yankees. Playing in front of 50 friends and family members, he went 3-for-4 in that game, hitting a double and two home runs. "It was unbelievable," Ramirez said later. "I remember I felt so funny in [my stomach], like the butterfly."

Ramirez in action against the Chicago White Sox, 1995.

Ramirez started spring training on the Indians major league roster in 1994. Nevertheless, team management expected the young Dominican to spend one more year at the Triple-A level before he could play full-time for the Indians. Although he had proven himself as a hitter, his defensive skills were not that strong. "But Manny came to me [in the spring] and said, 'I know I can make the club,'" Manager Mike Hargrove recalled. "And he worked very, very hard. And he turned things around for himself, where we just had to keep him." Ramirez went on to hit .269 with 17 home runs and 60 RBIs in the strike-shortened 1994 season, finishing second to the Kansas City Royals' Bob Hamelin in voting for Rookie of the Year.

In 1995, his first full season with the Tribe, Ramirez emerged as one of the most feared hitters in baseball. He batted .308 with 31 home runs and 107 RBIs in just 137 games. His performance earned him a spot on the American League All-Star team. More importantly, he led the Indians to the American League playoffs, where they knocked off the Boston Red Sox and the Seattle Mariners to make it to the World Series for the first time since 1954. Unfortunately, Cleveland lost the series to the talented Atlanta Braves, four games to two.

In 1996 Ramirez signed a four-year contract with the Indians. On the field, his numbers were nearly identical to the previous season: .309 batting average, 33 home runs, and 112 RBIs. The Indians again made the playoffs, but this time lost in the first round to the Baltimore Orioles. In 1997 his power numbers dropped to 25 home runs and 88 RBIs, but he averaged a career-best .328. Many analysts claimed that Ramirez had become a more disciplined hitter and improved his sense of the strike zone. "He's one of the few players I let swing with a 3-0 count [3 balls and no strikes]," said Hargrove. "And he doesn't swing wildly. If it's a ball, he lets it pass. A lot of young hitters wouldn't."

The Indians started the 1997 season as one of the favorites to win the World Series. The Tribe had it all that year — good hitting, strong pitching, solid fielding — and easily advanced through the playoffs to face the young and inexperienced Florida Marlins in the World Series. Unfortunately, the heavily favored Indians came up just short of winning their first world title since 1920.

In 1998 and 1999, a more mature Ramirez blossomed into arguably the best hitter in baseball. He posted two of the best back-to-back seasons in recent memory. In 1998 his average dipped a bit to .294, but he hit career highs in both home runs (45) and runs batted in (145). The following season Ramirez turned in his finest year yet, batting .333 with 174 hits, including 44 home runs. Most impressively, he knocked in 165 runs for the year, which was the most in the major leagues since Hall of Fame player Jimmie Foxx drove in 175 in 1938. Only eight players had ever had more RBIs in one season, and all of them are in the Major League Baseball Hall of Fame. "He's a magnificent hitter," said Anaheim Angels scout Joe McDonald. "He's got great bat control. I don't know how to pitch to the guy. He always has quality at-bats."

In 2000, the Indians' five-year streak of Central Division titles and postseason appearances came to an end. It was a difficult season for Ramirez, too, as an injury to his left hamstring forced him to miss six weeks of the season. But the fact that he missed 44 games only made his batting statistics for that year more incredible. In addition to reaching another career high in batting average with .351, he hit 38 home runs and drove in 122 runs — an average of more than one per game.

Signing with the Boston Red Sox

Indians fans and team management expected Ramirez to sign a new contract during the offseason that would keep the young star in Cleveland for many years to come. But he had other plans. He shocked many baseball insiders by signing an eight-year, $160 million free-agent contract with the

The newest member of the Boston Red Sox.

Boston Red Sox, a deal that made him one of the highest-paid players in all of sports.

Ramirez soon explained that a dispute with Indians management convinced him to seek a new team. He was upset that while he was on the disabled list during the 2000 season, several team officials had hinted to the media that they felt the star player was exaggerating his hamstring injury. For example, team owner Larry Dolan said during Ramirez's 44-game absence, "It doesn't look like he wants to help us."

"What they said hurt a lot," Ramirez stated. "Those people behaved badly. I'm in my last year [of my contract], and I don't want to play? That doesn't even fit in the mind of a crazy man. They didn't even ask me if I could play. . . . I was a calf raised on that farm, and I appreciate the opportunity they gave me, but they should be ashamed. They weren't thinking of me. They were thinking of themselves." Feeling angry and frustrated, Ramirez jumped at the Red Sox offer.

Another factor in Ramirez's decision to sign with the Red Sox was his desire to win a World Series. "I was tired of just winning division titles," he noted. "I want to win—really win." Although Boston had not won a

World Series title since 1918, the team was a perennial contender, locked in an annual battle with the New York Yankees for American League supremacy. Red Sox General Manager Dan Duquette believed that Ramirez could be the final piece of the puzzle that would lift the Sox past the Yankees. "He's one of the 10 most productive hitters in history," Duquette explained. "His best years are ahead of him. Combine slugging [percentage] and on-base percentage, and only names like Babe Ruth, Ted Williams, and Lou Gehrig are ahead of him."

Outside of Red Sox officials and fans, however, it was hard to find baseball analysts who supported the team's decision to acquire Ramirez. Many said that Boston had overpaid for a one-dimensional and sometimes quirky player. In his first three years in Boston, Ramirez continued to hit the ball as well as anyone in the game. In fact, he hit a home run in his first at-bat in Boston's Fenway Park in 2001. He went on to bat .306 with 41 home runs and 125 RBIs that season. His statistics were similar the following two years: in 2002 he batted .349 with 33 home runs and 107 RBIs; and in 2003 he hit .325 with 37 homers and knocked in 104 runs.

> "He's one of the 10 most productive hitters in history," said Red Sox General Manager Dan Duquette. "His best years are ahead of him. Combine slugging [percentage] and on-base percentage, and only names like Babe Ruth, Ted Williams, and Lou Gehrig are ahead of him."

Despite Ramirez's solid performances, however, the Red Sox missed the playoffs in 2001 and 2002. Although the team finally returned to the postseason as a wild-card team in 2003, they lost to their hated rivals, the Yankees, in the American League Championship Series (ALCS). As each of his first three seasons ended in disappointment, Ramirez felt increasing pressure to perform. Yet he also gave fans reason to question his commitment to winning. Although he was a great hitter, he sometimes made fielding or base-running blunders (such as forgetting how many outs there were in an inning). Such blunders made it appear he was not keeping his head in the game and providing his best effort at all times. Ramirez also became known for his unusual behavior both on and off the field. He once colored his hair bright red, for example, and he annoyed several of his teammates by borrowing their equipment without permission.

A Close Call

By the time the 2003 season concluded, Red Sox management had grown tired of Ramirez's flaky behavior. He had infuriated his teammates and manager Grady Little by sitting out a crucial late-season series against the Yankees because of a sore throat. During that same period, Ramirez had refused to pinch-hit during a game against the Philadelphia Phillies. Although he still claimed to be sick, he had skipped a doctor's appointment the day before the game. Little reacted by benching him for a game, with the full backing of Red Sox management.

Deciding that the team would be better off without him, the Red Sox placed Ramirez on waivers—meaning that any other team could claim him, without providing any players in trade, if they were willing to take over the $20 million annual salary that the Red Sox had agreed to pay him. Not surprisingly, no other team accepted that financial burden. The Red Sox also tried to trade him to the Texas Rangers for star shortstop Alex Rodriguez. But that deal fell through, so Ramirez remained with the Red Sox.

Despite his on-field mistakes and refusal to play through illness and injury, however, Ramirez remained popular among his teammates. In fact, every player on the Red Sox claimed that they were pleased to have him back in 2004. "He's a guy who gets misperceived around the media and stuff as this bad guy," said Boston all-purpose player Kevin Millar. "If you go around and ask the other 24 guys in this clubhouse, they'd tell you Manny is one of the greatest teammates you could ever have."

Battling the Yankees for the 2004 American League Championship

As the 2004 season began, Ramirez and his teammates put the tumultuous off-season behind them and focused on making the playoffs and winning the World Series. New Red Sox manager Terry Francona promised to give Ramirez a fresh start, noting that "all I heard was that he was a fabulous kid and that the other players loved him." Ramirez also benefitted from a close friendship with Millar, who helped the superstar to loosen up a bit and enjoy the game. "Now he's opening up a little bit to the outside world," Francona stated, "and that's good for everyone because now everyone gets to see a little bit of what his teammates have seen."

Once the season got underway, it became apparent that Boston was fielding its best team in years. Ramirez once again posted amazing offensive numbers, with a .308 average, 43 home runs, and 130 RBIs. His 43 round-trippers earned him the American League home run title for the first time

Ramirez leaps over the wall and reaches into the stands to take a home run away from the Yankees.

in his career, and he also led the league in slugging percentage at .613. The Red Sox fell just short of catching the Yankees to claim the American League East title, but Boston still managed to qualify for the playoffs as a wild-card team. The Red Sox then swept the Anaheim Angels in the first round to advance to the ALCS.

The American League Championship Series featured another highly antic-ipated showdown between the Red Sox and Yankees. At first, it looked as if another season was going to end in bitter disappointment for Boston. Appearing sluggish, the Red Sox lost the first three games of the best-of-seven series and faced near-certain elimination at the hands of their rivals. No team had ever come back from a 3-0 deficit to win a seven-game series in the century-long modern era of professional baseball, and no one ex-pected the Red Sox to become the first to accomplish the feat. Boston fans lamented that their team was once again falling victim to the infamous Curse of the Bambino—a curse that was supposedly placed on the Red Sox in 1920, when the team sold legendary star Babe Ruth to the Yankees. Ever since that trade, Boston fans desperate for a championship have cited the curse as the reason for the team's failure to win the World Series.

But instead of meekly standing aside for the Yankees, the Red Sox pulled together to launch one of the most miraculous comebacks in the history of

> ――― **"** ―――
>
> *"I never thought I'd get to be part of a World Series winner. Anything is possible. We proved we could win. We broke The Curse. I'm just so happy. I can't wait to go home and celebrate."*
>
> ――― **"** ―――

sports. Facing elimination in Game 4, the Red Sox came from behind to tie the game in the ninth inning. They went on to win, 6-4, on a two-run homer by David Ortiz in the 12th inning. Ortiz was the hero again the next day, hitting a single that gave the Sox a 5-4 victory in Game 5. In Game 6, Boston's ace pitcher Curt Schilling turned in one of the gutsiest performances in baseball history. He pitched six innings to lead his team to a 4-2 win over the Yankees, ignoring that fact that the stitches holding together a dislocated tendon in his ankle had torn out during the game, turning his sock into a bloody mess.

In the deciding Game 7, the Red Sox scored early and often to silence the Yankee Stadium crowd, and went on to crush the Yankees, 10–3. Red Sox General Manager Theo Epstein gushed that the Red Sox ALCS triumph was one for the ages. "There have been so many great Red Sox teams and players who would have tasted World Series champagne if it wasn't for the Yankees," he said in the raucous clubhouse after the game. "Guys in '49, and '78, and us last year. Now that we've won, this is for them. We can put that behind us and move on to the World Series and take care of that."

Becoming MVP of the 2004 World Series

Compared to the drama of the ALCS, the World Series seemed anticlimactic. Boston swept the St. Louis Cardinals in four straight games to win the team's first world championship in 87 years. After being held without

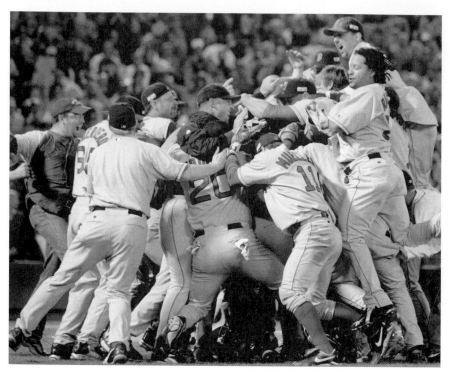

Ramirez (at right) and Red Sox teammates celebrate their World Series win over the Cardinals. It was the first Red Sox World Series win since 1918.

any RBIs in the ALCS, Ramirez emerged as the star of the World Series. He batted .412 (7-for-17) with a home run and 4 RBIs. He got at least one hit in all 14 games of the 2004 playoffs to extend his hitting streak in post-season games to 17, tying the all-time record held by Hank Bauer and Derek Jeter.

Though Ramirez has often been criticized for his defensive play in left field, he made a key play in the first inning of Game 3 against the Cardinals, throwing out Larry Walker at home plate when he tried to score on a shallow fly ball. Ramirez's catch-and-throw double play kept St. Louis off the scoreboard and ended the inning. Following the Red Sox sweep, Ramirez was named Most Valuable Player of the 2004 World Series. "I never thought I'd get to be part of a World Series winner," he said afterward. "Anything is possible. We proved we could win. We broke The Curse. I'm just so happy. I can't wait to go home and celebrate."

The entire city of Boston — along with long-suffering Red Sox fans from around the world — joined in the celebration. Ramirez later expressed his appreciation to the city and the team. "It was good for me to come [here]," he said. "The fans made me a better player. When I was in Cleveland, I never played like I do now. I wasn't focused. I was a good player, but I wasn't a great player like I am. That's something I will always like about Boston."

MARRIAGE AND FAMILY

Ramirez married Juliana Monterio, a native of Brazil who formerly worked as a hostess at a New York restaurant, in 2001. "My wife and I are a great combination," he said. "She's always there for me and I try to be there for her. It's unbelievable. I'm just blessed, man. That's why I'm always happy. Every day when I wake up, I thank God for everything I have." They live in a luxury penthouse apartment in Boston.

Ramirez and his wife have a son, Manny Jr., who was born in early 2003. Ramirez also has another son, Manuel, from a previous relationship. Manuel, who turned 10 in 2004, lives with his mother but enjoys regular visits with his father and stepmother. "My kids give me a tremendous amount of joy," Ramirez said. "They live apart, but when they spend time together, they connect. I'm looking forward to seeing them become close as they grow up."

"It was good for me to come [to Boston]," Ramirez said. "The fans made me a better player. When I was in Cleveland, I never played like I do now. I wasn't focused. I was a good player, but I wasn't a great player like I am. That's something I will always like about Boston."

HOBBIES AND OTHER INTERESTS

Ramirez is actively involved in numerous charitable endeavors, most of which benefit children. For example, he donates his time and money to the CHARLEE (Children Have Rights: Legal, Educational, Emotional) Homes for Children program, a Boston-area charity that helps abused children. In 2005 he announced that he was forming his own organization, the MR24 Foundation, to further aid children.

When the Dominican Republic suffered devastating floods in May 2004 that killed more than 2,000 people, Ramirez joined teammates and fellow Dominicans David Ortiz and Pedro Martinez in collecting donations from

Red Sox fans. The three players raised more than $200,000 to support relief efforts in the Dominican Republic and neighboring Haiti.

On May 10, 2004, Ramirez took a one-game leave of absence from the Red Sox in order to take an oath of citizenship in the United States. Ramirez decided to become an American citizen because it was important to his mother. He studied for more than a year to learn about the U.S. Constitution and system of government, and he passed the exam easily.

HONORS AND AWARDS

Appalachian League Most Valuable Player: 1991
Short Season Player of the Year (*Baseball America*): 1991
Minor League Player of the Year (*Baseball America*): 1993
American League All-Star Team: 1995, 1998-2004
Silver Slugger Award: 1995, 1999-2004
Man of the Year (Cleveland Indians): 1998, 1999
Athletic Hall of Fame (New York City Public Schools): 1999
Hank Aaron Award: 1999, 2004
World Series Most Valuable Player: 2004

FURTHER READING

Books

Egan, Terry, Stan Friedmann, and Mike Levine. *The Good Guys of Baseball: Sixteen True Sports Stories*, 1997 (juvenile)
Vascellero, Charlie. *Latinos in Baseball: Manny Ramirez*, 2000 (juvenile)

Periodicals

Boston Globe, Oct. 5, 2004, p.F4; Oct. 21, 2004, p.C1; Oct. 28, 2004, p.C8; Oct. 31, 2004, p.C4; Dec. 14, 2004, p.C5
Boston Herald, Nov. 9, 2001, p.8; Oct. 31, 2003, p.112; Oct. 17, 2004, p.B16
Boston Magazine, Nov. 2004
ESPN Magazine, Mar. 5, 2001
GQ, Sep. 2004, p.274
New York Daily News, Oct. 24, 2004, p.70
New York Times, June 3, 1991, p.B1, June 4, 1991, p.B4; June 18, 1995, p.H1; Sep. 23, 1997, p.C1; Oct. 25, 2004, p.A1; Nov. 2, 2004, p.D4
Sport, Aug. 2000, p.40
Sporting News, Mar. 9, 1998, p.40; Nov. 13, 2000, p.64; July 2, 2001, p.10; Sep. 15, 2003, p.24

Sports Illustrated, July 10, 1995, p.24; Apr. 5, 1999, p.62; Oct. 11, 1999, p.38;
   Oct. 2, 2000, p.112; June 4, 2001, p.54; July 7, 2004, p.56
Sports Illustrated for Kids, Sep. 1999, p.66; Sep. 2001, p.82
USA Today, Oct. 27, 2004, p.C4

Online Articles

http://www.boston.com/sports
   (*Boston.com*, "Ramirez Misses First Game of Year to Become U.S.
   Citizen,"May 10, 2004)

Online Databases

Biography Resource Center Online, 2005

ADDRESS

Manny Ramirez
Boston Red Sox
4 Yawkey Way
Fenway Park
Boston, MA 02215

WORLD WIDE WEB SITES

http://www.mannyramirez.com
http://redsox.mlb.com
http://cbs.sportsline.com/mlb/players
http://sports.espn.go.com
http://www.bigleaguers.com

Vijay Singh 1963-

Fijian Golfer
2004 PGA Tour Player of the Year

BIRTH

Vijay Kumar Singh was born on February 22, 1963, in Lautoka, Fiji. Fiji is an island nation in the South Pacific, near New Zealand and Australia. His father, Mohan Singh, was an airport technician and part-time golf instructor. He and Vijay's mother, Parawati Singh, are no longer together. Vijay has five brothers and sisters. His first name, which is pronounced VEE-jay, means "victory" in the Hindi language.

YOUTH

Although Vijay grew up on Fiji, his ancestors came from India. Since the first Indian immigrants to Fiji were poor laborers who worked in the sugar-cane fields, native Fijians have long considered Indians to be second-class citizens. Like many other Fijians of Indian descent, Vijay and his family often were the victims of discrimination.

The Singh family moved to the town of Nadi when Vijay was very young. They lived in a modest house near the nine-hole Nadi Airport Golf Club. In addition to working at the airport, Mohan Singh was an avid amateur golfer. He gave lessons at the Nadi course and won the club championship nine times. Vijay often served as a caddie for his father, who taught him the basics of the game.

When Vijay was eight years old, his father gave him a set of used golf clubs. The sport soon became his passion. In fact, he often upset his father by skipping school to play golf. Sometimes he became so eager to practice that rather than wait for a bus to transport him around the Nadi Airport, he would race across the runways to get to the golf course. Vijay spent so much time on the practice grounds as a boy that the Nadi course named the facility after him in the early 1990s. He also worked as a caddie at the course for $1 a day.

—————— " ——————

"There was nothing going on for me on Fiji," Singh recalled. "You could get a job, but you could hardly make a living out of it. I just wanted to play golf, and the only way to do that was to get out."

—————— " ——————

By 1979, 16-year-old Vijay had become the best golfer on Fiji. He then decided that he needed to leave the island in order to take his game to the next level. "There was nothing going on for me on Fiji," he recalled. "You could get a job, but you could hardly make a living out of it. I just wanted to play golf, and the only way to do that was to get out." Vijay quit school and traveled to Australia in hopes of making a career as a professional golfer.

CAREER HIGHLIGHTS

Facing Early Setbacks

After moving to Australia, Singh spent three years playing in amateur golf tournaments before he accumulated enough top-10 finishes to become a professional golfer. But the 19-year-old soon realized that the level of pro-

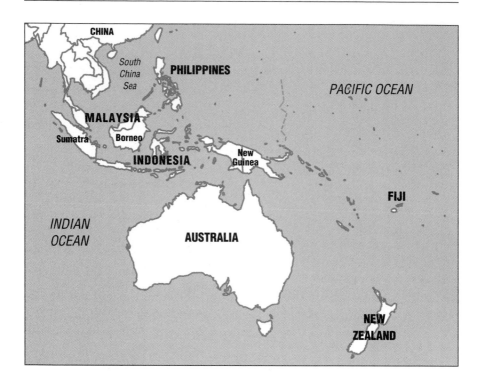

fessional competition was much higher in Australia than it had been on Fiji. To his great disappointment, he found that he was not good enough to qualify for the Australian Professional Golfers Association (PGA) tour. "The standard of golf was so much higher," he remembered. "I didn't know where the ball was going. I didn't have any idea of what the golf swing was."

Determined to gain more experience, Singh practiced constantly and made steady improvement. He eventually qualified for the Australian PGA tour and started winning some tournaments, but he still did not earn enough money to make a career in the sport. To make ends meet, Singh borrowed money and made long-distance calls using clubhouse telephones. His financial situation finally became so bad that he was banned from the Australian PGA tour for unpaid debts and outstanding phone bills. It would be years before he could repay what he owed.

After being banned from the Australian PGA tour, Singh moved to the Southeast Asian country of Malaysia, where he found work teaching golf. He also qualified for the Malaysian PGA tour, and in 1984 he won the tour championship. The following year he married one of his golf students, Adrena Seth. They eventually had a son together, Qass Seth Singh.

Hitting Rock Bottom

Singh's professional reputation suffered another blow during the 1985 Indonesian Open, when tournament officials and fellow players accused him of cheating. They claimed that he had altered his second-round scorecard, lowering his total score by one stroke, in order to make the cutoff and continue playing in the tournament. He denied the charges, insisting that another player had recorded his score incorrectly. Nevertheless, Singh was banned from the Asian professional tour and from the Southeast Asia Golf Federation over the incident.

Singh was an immature, struggling 22-year-old at the time this incident occurred. He has not been accused of anything similar since, yet the allegations that he cheated have dogged him throughout his career. He has long refused to discuss the matter publicly, and he has admitted feeling anger toward the media for continuing to mention it years later. "Why should I admit to cheating, even 15 years ago, if I didn't?" he once said. "Just so you people in the press won't keep bringing it up? I cannot do that. That would be dishonest in itself."

———— " ————

"I was out there in the jungle, hitting balls in the 100-degree heat and trying to think about what I'm going to do next," Singh recalled. "That was the lowest point. I don't even like to think about it. I never thought about coming to America, let alone winning a golf tournament here."

———— " ————

Upon finding himself on the outside of professional golf once again, Singh moved to the Southeast Asian island of Borneo. He spent the next two years working as a golf pro at the Keningau Golf Club, where he earned $160 per week. Keningau was a remote and lonely place in the middle of a rainforest, more than two hours' drive from the nearest city. Singh found it difficult to imagine ever making it back to the world of professional golf. "I was out there in the jungle, hitting balls in the 100-degree heat and trying to think about what I'm going to do next," he recalled. "That was the lowest point. I don't even like to think about it. I never thought about coming to America, let alone winning a golf tournament here."

Through hard work and dedication, Singh managed to overcome his early setbacks. He practiced diligently to improve his game and reflected on his mistakes in order to learn from them. He emerged from his exile in Borneo "a little more polished and a lot more mature," he noted. "An experience like that forces you to grow up."

In 1988, at the age of 25, Singh qualified for Africa's Safari Tour. His return to professional golf went well enough that he was invited to join the European PGA tour the following year. He claimed his first victory on the European PGA tour in only the sixth event he entered, the Volvo Open in Sardinia, Italy. Singh went on to notch three more wins in his first four years on the European tour. His success gave him hope of eventually qualifying to play on the most prestigious professional golf tour in the world, the American PGA. "The dream is to play in America," he acknowledged. "It is the ultimate Tour."

His success on the European PGA tour gave him hope of eventually qualifying to play on the most prestigious professional golf tour in the world, the American PGA. "The dream is to play in America," Singh acknowledged. "It is the ultimate Tour."

Joining the American PGA Tour

Singh played his first match in the United States—the Memorial Tournament—in 1992, at the invitation of golf legend Jack Nicklaus. He finished an impressive seventh at the Memorial, and a week later he placed 13th in the Federal Express St. Jude Classic. Singh ended up taking home a respectable $70,680 in winnings that year. His record of consistently solid performances helped him earn a coveted spot on the American PGA Tour in 1993.

Singh made an immediate splash on the tour in 1993 by winning the first tournament he entered—the Buick Classic—beating Mark Weibe on the third hole of a sudden-death tiebreaker. He went on to finish in the top 10 in six tournaments and ended the season ranked 19th in earnings, with $657,000. In recognition of his performance, the PGA named him 1993 Rookie of the Year.

Unfortunately, Singh was not able to maintain his strong showing in 1994. Back and neck problems kept him out of several matches and cut his previous year's winnings in half. Although he placed second in two tournaments, he only managed to break into the top 10 in one other event that year. But Singh staged a comeback in 1995, winning the Phoenix Open and the Buick Classic and placing in the top 10 in several other matches. His earnings for the year topped $1 million.

Singh failed to win a tournament in 1996, but he played consistently enough to finish in the top 10 nine times and win $855,000. He came back to win four events in 1997 — the Memorial Tournament, Buick Open, South African Open, and World Match Play — and once again topped $1 million in prize money for the year.

Winning the 1998 PGA Championship

By 1998, Singh had come a long way since being banned by the Australian PGA for unpaid phone bills. He had won five events on the PGA tour, as well as numerous international tournaments, and established himself as one of the world's elite golfers. Partly due to his reluctance to grant media interviews, however, he had not gained widespread recognition outside of the world of golf. Reporters described him as

Singh in action at the 1998 PGA Championship, on the way to capturing his first major title.

aloof, standoffish, distant, and even rude. Tim Cowlishaw, a writer for the *Dallas Morning News,* argued that Singh kept reporters at arm's length because they continued to focus on allegations that he had cheated in Indonesia more than a decade earlier. "Perhaps it's time to leave Singh's past in the past," Cowlishaw wrote. "His present is intriguing enough."

In order to be considered among the best in his sport, Singh knew that he needed to win a "major" event on the PGA Tour. There are four major PGA tournaments, also known as "Grand Slam" events: the British Open, the U.S. Open, the PGA Championship, and the Masters. These are viewed as the most prestigious golf contests in the world. Singh succeeded in capturing his first major at the 1998 PGA Championship, held at the Sahalee Country Club near Seattle, Washington. A week later, he showed that the major win was no fluke by edging out a number of top golfers to win the Sprint International tournament.

Singh finished the 1998 season with more than $2.2 million in earnings, which ranked among the top players in the game that year. He topped $2 million in earnings again in 1999. He claimed his eighth career victory on the PGA Tour — and his fifth in two years — at the Honda Classic, and also made strong showings in a number of other tournaments.

Changing People's Minds at the 2000 Masters

Despite his strong performances in 1998 and 1999, Singh still found himself playing in the shadow of more popular players, particularly Tiger Woods. Woods had emerged as the dominant player in the game during that time, finishing first or second in 10 of the previous 11 tournaments he had entered leading up to the 2000 Masters. The media relegated Singh to the group of "second-best" players who were looking for a way to beat Woods. (For more information on Woods, see *Biography Today Sports*, Vols. 1 & 6, and Update in *Biography Today Annual Cumulation*, 2000.)

Singh set out to challenge that record in the 2000 Masters. Many fans consider the Masters to be the most prestigious, and the most difficult, contest in professional golf. It takes place in Augusta, Georgia, on a course that is legendary for its long fairways and fast greens. To be successful there, players must not only hit long, accurate drives, but also possess a delicate and precise touch with the putter. Singh prepared for the tournament by concentrating on his putting, which had never been the best part of his game. He switched to a new putter and also consulted books for advice on conquering the mental aspect of the short game. "I've decided to try enjoying putting more than hating it," he explained. "If I have a bad attitude on the greens, I may as well not come here."

> "For the past two decades he has been the game's international man of mystery, collecting victories on five continents but precious few supporters along the way," Alan Shipnuck wrote in **Sports Illustrated**. "Singh was long ago written off by reporters as the worst interview in the sport, and even the most respectful of golf fans have remained indifferent to him. ... Perhaps with his joyous Masters victory Singh will finally feel comfortable introducing a kinder, gentler version of himself to the golfing public."

As Singh prepared to play his first-round match at the Masters, he found a note from his son in his golf bag that read: "Dad, trust your swing." Inspired by Qass's advice, Singh played well throughout the tournament and carried a three-shot lead over David Duval into the final round. Although Duval closed the gap to one stroke at one point, Singh managed

Singh's impressive performance at the 2000 Masters earned him new respect from the media and golf fans.

to pull away again. Practically assured of victory as he approached the green on the 18th hole, Singh received polite applause from most of the gallery. But television cameras focused instead on a boisterous group of more than a dozen friends and family members that followed him down the final fairway shouting encouragement, hugging each other, and crying tears of joy. "It's an incredibly warm feeling," he said after winning his second career major. "I have never felt more accepted, or more at home."

Singh's impressive three-stroke victory at the 2000 Masters helped change his image in the eyes of golf fans and the media. "For the past two decades he has been the game's international man of mystery, collecting victories on five continents but precious few supporters along the way," Alan Shipnuck wrote in *Sports Illustrated*. "Singh was long ago written off by reporters as the worst interview in the sport, and even the most respectful of golf fans have remained indifferent to him. . . . Perhaps with his joyous Masters victory Singh will finally feel comfortable introducing a kinder, gentler version of himself to the golfing public." That view was echoed by fellow professional golfer Loren Roberts. "He's a great champion, a deserving champion," Roberts said. "I think a lot of people misunderstand

Vijay. He's not aloof, but genuine. . . . Above all, Vijay loves the game and respects the game, and that is evident in his dedication to improving and in the way he conducts himself."

Singh's triumph at the Masters marked the beginning of an outstanding 2000 season. He finished in the top 10 in 12 of the 16 tournaments he entered. By the end of the year, he was the sixth-ranked golfer in the world. Although Singh failed to win a tournament in 2001 for the first time in five years, he collected 14 top-10 finishes and ended the season ranked fourth on the money list, with $3.4 million in earnings. He returned to the victory circle twice in 2002, winning the Shell Houston Open and the TOUR Championship. He finished the season with $3.7 million in winnings to rank third on the 2002 money list.

> "He's a great champion, a deserving champion," said fellow professional golfer Loren Roberts. "I think a lot of people misunderstand Vijay. He's not aloof, but genuine. . . . Above all, Vijay loves the game and respects the game, and that is evident in his dedication to improving and in the way he conducts himself."

Creating More Controversy

In 2003 Singh posted the best year of his career, with 18 top-10 finishes and four tournament championships. He earned $7.5 million to claim the PGA Tour money title for the first time in his career, and he barely missed winning PGA Player of the Year honors. Instead, the coveted award went to Tiger Woods for the fifth straight year.

Unfortunately, Singh also became involved in a new controversy that overshadowed his excellent performances on the links in 2003. In the middle of that season, the female golfer Annika Sorenstam announced her intention to play in an event on the PGA Tour, the Bank of America Colonial Tournament. A dominant player on the Ladies' PGA Tour, Sorenstam was the top-ranked female golfer in the world, and many fans were curious to see how she would fare in a competition against men. When she agreed to play in the Colonial, it marked the first appearance by a woman on the Men's Tour since 1945. (For more information on Sorenstam, see *Biography Today Sports*, Vol. 6.)

When a reporter asked Singh about Sorenstam's plan to play in the Colonial, he replied, "I hope she misses the [qualifying round] cut. Why? Because she doesn't belong there." Singh went on to express his opinion that women should stick to their own league, and he also threatened to withdraw from the tournament if he were paired with Sorenstam. His comments created a firestorm of protest from fans and the media. Outraged journalists published articles calling him a "sexist oaf," a "sinister pig," "Vijay the Villain," and "the Fleein' Fijian."

During the intense media attention that followed Singh's comments about Sorenstam, a number of reporters dredged up the controversies that had surrounded Singh in the past, including the debt issues in Australia and the cheating scandal in Indonesia. Singh felt that bringing up problems from the distant past was unfair, and the dust-up revived his distrust of the press. "Those things kind of hurt me," he admitted.

Several of Singh's friends on the PGA Tour came to his defense. "I can't imagine how frustrating it would be to do something good and hear, 'Yeah, but he's a cheater.' All because of some murky thing from overseas that, no matter what happened, is over and done," said fellow player Dan Forsman. "The guy's been a great champion since then, and to me, you can't have a cheater's mentality and be a great champion. So it's unfair to keep bringing it up to take away all that he's achieved."

Breaking Records in 2004

In 2004 Singh overcame the controversy to turn in one of the finest seasons in the history of golf. He won nine PGA tournaments and set a new record for single-season earnings with $10.9 million. He became the first golfer ever to win more than $10 million in a season, and only the sixth player in tour history to win nine or more tournaments in a year. Although Tiger Woods had accomplished the feat in 2000, the last player to do so before that had been Sam Snead in 1950. "Most of the players on tour never thought anybody else would win nine times, other than Tiger," PGA player Stewart Cink stated. "What it does is give everybody else hope, that it could be one of us one day."

The highlight of Singh's 2004 season came when he won his third career major at the PGA Championship in August. Although he entered the final round with a one-stroke lead over Justin Leonard, Singh played poorly over the last 18 holes. But Leonard was unable to close him out, and the two golfers finished in a three-way tie for first place with Chris DiMarco. In the sudden-death playoff round that followed, Singh regained his form and made several bold shots to claim a one-stroke victory. Afterward, some people suggested that it was the ugliest win of his career, but Singh disagreed. "It's the prettiest one, I think. I just hung in there. I never gave up," he stated. "I think this is the biggest accomplishment I've ever had in

Winning the 2004 PGA Championship was the highlight of Singh's season.

my career." It marked his 20th win on the PGA Tour, to go along with 22 international victories.

In September 2004 Singh overtook Tiger Woods as the world's top-ranked golfer. At the end of the season he was crowned PGA Player of the Year, breaking Woods's five-year hold on the honor. "It's been a big year," Singh said after receiving the award. "I never thought it would be this big. It's so satisfying to know that it has come to this. It was well worth the journey."

Staying on Top

By the end of the 2004 season, Singh's career winnings exceeded $40 million. After posting top-10 finishes in 12 consecutive tournaments in 2003 and 2004, he has earned a reputation as one of the most consistent players on the tour. Still, he knows that his success will make him a marked man in the 2005 season. "They say it's really hard to get to the top, but to stay there is going to be the hardest thing," he noted. "I feel like I'm on an open plain and all you see is the horizon. I feel like I'm running and everybody is chasing me. Sooner or later, I'm going to get tired and guys are going to catch me. So I want to stay there. I want to keep ahead of the pack for as long as possible."

In early 2005 Singh was elected to the World Golf Hall of Fame. "This is a great story, a story about a player who came from a fairly humble start to rise to the pinnacle of this sport," PGA Tour Commissioner Tim Finchem said in announcing Singh's election. "It's an amazing honor to be part of an incredible group that is in the Hall of Fame," he noted. "There are no words to describe it. I'm honored, and I'd like to thank everyone that helped me along the way."

Singh is often referred to as "golf's hardest worker" by his fellow players. He spends countless hours at the practice range, hitting between 500 and 1000 balls most days. Mick Elliott of the *Tampa Tribune* described Singh as the "ultimate practice machine." "He's got an unyielding desire to be the best he can be," added his former caddie, Paul Tesori.

> *"They say it's really hard to get to the top, but to stay there is going to be the hardest thing," Singh noted. "I feel like I'm on an open plain and all you see is the horizon. I feel like I'm running and everybody is chasing me. Sooner or later, I'm going to get tired and guys are going to catch me. So I want to stay there. I want to keep ahead of the pack for as long as possible."*

Now in his 40s, Singh still maintains an intense training schedule. Six days a week, he rises before dawn to work out with his personal trainer in a private gym that adjoins his home. He plays golf every afternoon, then returns to the gym for a second workout. "The guy is built like a tight end, and the way his body is holding up, I don't see him slowing down at all," said fellow player David Toms. "He's got the respect of all of us."

The strongest point of Singh's game is his tee shot, and he is often compared to the greatest ball-strikers in history with his long, fluid swing. In fact, his fellow golfers have nicknamed him "Vijay Swing." From the beginning of his career, Singh has studied photographs and videotapes of

Tom Weiskopf and other top players in order to perfect his swing. "He's got the perfect body for golf," said golfer Paul Azinger. "His swing has great rhythm, and he has absolutely the right work ethic."

In the next few years, Singh hopes to win the U.S. Open and British Open in order to achieve a career Grand Slam. His approach to the game has always been simple. "I just play," he stated. "I hit a shot and wait for the next guy to hit his. I don't think between shots. That is my nature. Golf is a passion that will stay with me forever. It's all I know."

"I just play," Singh stated. "I hit a shot and wait for the next guy to hit his. I don't think between shots. That is my nature. Golf is a passion that will stay with me forever. It's all I know."

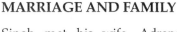

MARRIAGE AND FAMILY

Singh met his wife, Adrena Seth, while he was teaching golf in Malaysia. They married in 1985 and had a son, Qass Seth Singh, in 1990. Upon winning the PGA Player of the Year Award in 2004, Singh gave an emotional speech thanking his wife for her support throughout his career. "All the years of looking out [for me] in Asia, in Africa, in Europe. The hot weather in Borneo," he said. "And to be here, right now, where I am. . . . Honey, this is for you."

Singh has passed on his love of golf to his son, Qass, who has developed a loose, graceful swing like his father's. "I love this kid to death, and I just want to have the joy of seeing him hit golf shots," Singh noted. When asked if he hopes his son will also become a professional golfer, Singh replied: "I'm not going to force him. If he wants to be a player or a pro, I'll nudge him along, but I think he's got enough talent. He's only 14. You don't want him to lose interest at 18 or 19, because he has played too much."

The Singhs live with their six German shepherds in an oceanfront mansion in Ponte Vedra Beach, Florida. They also own a second home in London.

HOBBIES AND OTHER INTERESTS

In his spare time, Singh enjoys playing cricket, rugby, and snooker. He is also fond of James Bond movies and the musical group Fleetwood Mac.

Singh has become involved in golf course design. He has designed and built two courses in Asia, including one at the Mission Hills Resort in

Singh playing with his son, Qass Seth Singh.

Shenzhen, China, and is also helping to build a course in his hometown of Nadi, Fiji.

Singh is also active in charity work. He founded the Vijay Singh Charitable Foundation, which provides assistance to victims of domestic violence. In 2004 he donated $150,000 to the American Red Cross's Florida hurricane relief efforts.

HONORS AND AWARDS

PGA Tour Rookie of the Year: 1993
PGA Championship: 1998, 2004
Masters Championship: 2000
PGA Tour Money Leader: 2003, 2004
PGA Tour Player of the Year: 2004
World Golf Hall of Fame: 2005

FURTHER READING

Books

Who's Who in America, 2005

Periodicals

Chicago Sun-Times, June 27, 2004, p.92
Detroit News, Apr. 27, 2005, p.C4
ESPN Magazine, Apr. 11, 2005, p.116
Golf Digest, June 2000, p.247; Jan. 2004, p.76
Golf Magazine, Sep. 1993, p.50
Golf World, Apr. 14, 2000, p.28; Jan. 31, 2003, p.12
Independent (London), Oct. 8, 1992, p.38
Los Angeles Times, Nov. 20, 2003, p.S2
New York Times, Nov. 7, 2004, Golf, p.1
Orlando Sentinel, May 13, 2003, p. D1; Nov. 4, 2004, p.D3; Dec. 5, 2004, p.C14; Dec. 7, 2004, p.D3
Sports Illustrated, Aug. 24, 1998, p.32; Apr. 17, 2000, p.32; May 22, 2000, p.24; Feb. 3, 2003, p.9; June 23, 2003, p.15; Mar. 23, 2004, p.36; Aug. 23, 2004, p.70; Nov. 29, 2004, p.82
Times (London), Apr. 4, 1989
USA Today, Nov. 4, 2004, p.C9

Online Databases

Biography Resource Center Online, 2005

ADDRESS

Vijay Singh
South Florida PGA
10804 West Sample Road
Coral Springs, FL 33065-2632

WORLD WIDE WEB SITE

http://www.pgatour.com

Kerri Walsh 1978-

American Beach Volleyball Player
Winner of a Gold Medal in Beach Volleyball at the
2004 Olympic Games

BIRTH

Kerri Walsh was born on August 15, 1978, in Santa Clara, California. She was the second of four children born to Tim and Margie Walsh. She has an older brother, Marte, and two younger sisters, Kelli and K.C.

YOUTH

Kerri Walsh was born into a very athletic family. Her father played minor league baseball, and her mother was a standout volleyball player at Santa Clara University. Kerri shared her family's love of sports from an early age. She always tagged along with her brother to neighborhood sporting events, and she started playing tee-ball on a team coached by her father when she was just five years old. Despite the fact that she was the only girl in the league, Kerri became an all-star baseball player.

With guidance from her mother, Walsh began playing indoor volleyball in the fifth grade. Around this time, a doctor told her that she would end up being around 5 feet, 8 inches tall as an adult. Kerri was very upset to hear this prediction. Since her father was 6 feet, 8 inches tall, she had always hoped to be over 6 feet tall. She worried that being shorter than 6 feet might hinder her athletic goals (as it turned out, she grew to be 6 feet, 3 inches tall).

Walsh continued to play competitive volleyball throughout her youth. Regulation indoor volleyball features two teams, each of which consists of six players. The six players are arranged in two rows of three. The front-row players, who are closest to the net, are generally considered offensive players, while the back-row players are considered defensive players. The object of the game is to score points by making the ball hit the floor on the opposing team's side of the net. Each team must return the ball to the other side of the net using three or fewer hits. The first hit is called a dig (a defensive save) or pass; the second hit is called a set; and the third hit is called a spike. Hits or spikes that cannot be returned by the defensive team are called kills. The setter on the team is responsible for directing a team's offense. She receives the pass from a back-row defensive player and then uses the second hit to "set" (direct) the ball to a front-row player for a spike (third hit). Walsh took advantage of her height to become a powerful offensive hitter, but she also developed her defensive and setting skills in order to become a solid all-around player.

EDUCATION

Walsh attended Archbishop Mitty High in San Jose, California. She was tall, skinny, and shy, but she was also an outstanding two-sport athlete. In volleyball, she led her team to three state championships. In 1994 she was the only junior to win first-team high school all-American honors, as well as the only junior (and one of only four high school players) invited to participate in the U.S. Olympic Festival in Colorado Springs, Colorado. She was also named California high school athlete of the year that season.

During her senior season, Walsh tallied 516 kills, 283 digs, 177 blocks, and 48 serving aces. She was honored as California athlete of the year for the second time and was also named national high school volleyball player of the year for 1995. The national award was an especially big honor for Walsh. "Winning this award is very special and exciting because there are so many great volleyball players across the country. Now, I just want to have a good college career and hope I get noticed so I can get a tryout for the 2000 Olympics." In addition to her high school career, Walsh played for Team Mizuno of the United States Volleyball Association (USVA) and helped her team claim the 18-and-under national title.

Walsh was also a standout on the basketball court during her high school years. She played on Archbishop Mitty's varsity basketball team all four years, leading her team to four Central Coast Sectional titles, three Northern California titles, and the 1995 state championship. Walsh averaged 22.5 points, 14.5 rebounds, 4 blocks, and 4 steals per game during her senior year. By the time she graduated in 1995, Walsh had received several offers of college basketball scholarships. But she decided to play volleyball at Stanford University, where she had assisted the women's team as a ball girl and attended youth training camps for many years.

"Winning this award is very special and exciting because there are so many great volleyball players across the country," Walsh said about being named national high school volleyball player of the year for 1995. "Now, I just want to have a good college career and hope I get noticed so I can get a tryout for the 2000 Olympics."

College — The Stanford University Cardinal

Walsh majored in American Studies at Stanford, earning a bachelor's degree in 1999. She made an impact on the volleyball court from the beginning of her freshman year, immediately taking over the team lead in blocks, kills (with 4.76 per game), serving aces (.41) and digs (2.83). Opposing coaches began to take notice of the imposing Stanford freshman hitter. "She's a great player," said Colorado State Coach Rich Feller. "She's big, aggressive, athletic, and knows the game." UCLA Coach Andy Banachowski added that "she has a long arm she cracks like a whip, so she really hammers the ball. She's the best freshman I can recall in a lot of years."

153

Walsh playing for the Stanford Cardinal.

At Stanford, Walsh was surrounded by such talented players as Kristin Folkl, who went on to play professional basketball in the WNBA, and Logan Tom, who played for the U.S. Olympic Volleyball Team. Walsh was quick to credit her teammates for her success. "I'm doing so well because I'm on a great team," she said. "Opponents can't concentrate on me. I'm very fortunate. I came into an ideal situation." The Cardinal team won back-to-back NCAA Championships in the 1996 and 1997 seasons. They made it to the NCAA finals once again in 1998, but they lost the championship to undefeated Long Beach State. As it happened, the setter for Long Beach State was 1998 NCAA Player of the Year Misty May, who would eventually become Walsh's partner in beach volleyball.

Even on her top-notch Stanford team, Walsh still managed to stand out. She became only the second player in NCAA history to earn first-team all-American honors for all four years of her college career. She accomplished this feat despite being forced to switch positions during her sophomore year. Walsh had suffered a torn rotator cuff in her right shoulder during her senior year of high school. By her sophomore year of college, the pain from the injury was so severe that she could not spike a volleyball. Instead of sitting out a season, however, she switched to the setter position and served with her left hand. She ended up having two off-season surgeries to repair her shoulder. Walsh finished her college career with 1,500 kills, 1,200 digs, and 500 blocks. She is widely considered one of the best all-around college volleyball players ever.

CAREER HIGHLIGHTS

Playing Indoors at the Olympics

Following her outstanding college volleyball career, Walsh was invited to play for the U.S. National Women's Volleyball Team, which represents the country in international competitions, like the Olympic Games. Along with her Stanford teammate Logan Tom, she ended up making the indoor volleyball team that played for the United States at the 2000 Olympic Games in Sydney, Australia. The American women beat South Korea to get to the quarterfinals, where they lost to Russia. Although the Americans finished out of the medals in fourth place, this result was better than many people had anticipated.

It was at the 2000 Olympics that Walsh's volleyball career took an unexpected turn. Walsh's parents came to Sydney to watch her play. While there, they happened to meet Butch and Barbara May, the parents of Misty May. Butch May had been a member of the U.S. Men's Volleyball Team that competed in the 1968 Olympic Games. His daughter Misty was a world-class setter who had played against Walsh in high school and college. After leading Long Beach State to the NCAA title over Walsh's Stanford Cardinal, however, Misty May had turned professional and joined the beach volleyball tour. Teamed with experienced pro Holly McPeak, May made her beach volleyball debut in 2000 and went on to chalk up the most first-season wins of any player in U.S. history.

—— " ——

"I'm doing so well because I'm on a great team," Walsh said about her successful freshman year at Stanford. "Opponents can't concentrate on me. I'm very fortunate. I came into an ideal situation."

—— " ——

The beach volleyball team of May and McPeak qualified for the 2000 Olympics in the relatively new sport of beach volleyball, which had made its debut at the 1996 Games. In contrast to regulation volleyball, beach volleyball is played outdoors on a sand court and features only two players per team. A match concludes when one team wins two out of three games to 21 points. Competitors in beach volleyball tend to be very well-rounded, since they must contend with such factors as sun, wind, and variations in the playing surface. As a result of these factors, beach volleyball players rely more on quickness, positioning, and touch than raw hitting power.

Although May and McPeak had entered the 2000 Games as strong contenders, they finished a disappointing fifth in the Olympic tournament. Afterward, May began looking for a new partner. She decided that playing with an established teammate like McPeak so early in her career had placed her under too much pressure. May's parents discussed the situation with Walsh's parents and suggested that Kerri take up beach volleyball, which she had never played before. "Barb and I knew that somewhere in that long, spider-like body, she had all the makings of a great partner," Butch May recalled. Tim and Margie Walsh knew that their daughter was feeling burned out on indoor volleyball. Once the Olympics were over, they encouraged Kerri to get in touch with Misty May.

———— " ————

"Although I have been playing volleyball since I was 10 years old, it was only in my 22nd year that I attempted to play beach volleyball," Walsh said afterward. "I assure you, my 22nd year was one of the most challenging and humbling years of my life. Patience is a huge MUST! Be patient with yourself, put in your time, and good things will come."

———— " ————

Despite the fact that the two are only a year apart in age, Walsh had always looked up to May. In fact, when the women played against each other in high school, Walsh had asked May to autograph a towel. Walsh was excited about the opportunity to team up with May in beach volleyball. Although May is only 5 feet, 9 inches tall, she is a strong setter and jumper. In addition, forming a team gave both women a chance to learn the game of beach volleyball in a gradual, equal manner.

Moving Outdoors

Walsh and May first played outdoors together in January 2001. Walsh looked out of place in the beginning, as she adjusted to the two-person game. "It was like a traveling circus," she said of her early days in beach volleyball. "We kind of figured things out by trial and error." But Walsh showed natural talent and quickly established a reputation in the beach community for her ability to block and cover the court on defense. Her defensive skills, which were unusual for such a tall player, gave her team an immediate advantage in the two-person game.

Playing in international events sponsored by the Federation Internationale de Volleyball (FIVB), Walsh and May improved quickly and rose to fifth in the world rankings during the 2001 season. The following year they won five tournament championships out of 11 FIVB events to claim the top spot in the world rankings and win over $320,000 in prize money. "Although I have been playing volleyball since I was 10 years old, it was only in my 22nd year that I attempted to play beach volleyball," Walsh said

Walsh (left) with teammate Misty May (right).

afterward. "I assure you, my 22nd year was one of the most challenging and humbling years of my life. Patience is a huge MUST! Be patient with yourself, put in your time, and good things will come."

In 2003 Walsh and May continued playing in international events sponsored by FIVB and also began playing in American events sponsored by the Association of Volleyball Professionals (AVP). This marked the first year in which victories on the American AVP tour counted toward the world rankings and helped determine which beach volleyball teams would qualify for the Olympics (before this time, only teams' performance in FIVB events counted toward Olympic qualification). In Walsh and May's AVP debut, at the Paul Mitchell Fort Lauderdale Open, they beat the top-seeded team of Holly McPeak and Elaine Youngs to claim the tournament title.

> "I have never been one to take the microphone and verbally lead the charge, so this new job [as women's player representative to the FIVB World Tour] makes me very nervous," Walsh admitted. "However, I also see an opportunity to grow as an individual by pushing myself out of my comfort zone, as well as an opportunity to become more involved in the growth of beach volleyball around the world."

Walsh and May ended up going undefeated in AVP competition in 2003, finishing the series with 26 match victories. In the season finale, at the Beach Volleyball World Championships, they beat Brazil's Adriana Behar and Shelda Bede in two close games to become the first Americans ever to win the prestigious tournament. They were named AVP team of the year, and Walsh was honored as AVP Player of the Year. Their success continued during the FIVB season, when they won five tournaments and finished second and third in two others. Walsh and May finished the season ranked second in the world behind Bede and Behar.

Following her outstanding 2003 season in beach volleyball, Walsh was named as one of the two women's player representatives to the FIVB World Tour. Her responsibilities as a player representative included growing the sport by encouraging positive changes in how the game was governed and played. "I have never been one to take the microphone and verbally lead the charge, so this new job makes me very nervous," Walsh admitted. "However,

I also see an opportunity to grow as an individual by pushing myself out of my comfort zone, as well as an opportunity to become more involved in the growth of beach volleyball around the world."

As the 2004 Olympic Games approached, Walsh and May emerged as the most dominant team in women's beach volleyball. Beginning in July 2003, the pair went on an amazing winning streak that saw them claim 90 straight match victories and 15 consecutive tournament championships. After winning every event they entered for nearly a year, the team finally lost in June 2004 in the semifinals of the Manhattan Beach Open, to Annett Davis and Jenny Johnson. Not coincidentally, May had suffered an abdominal injury and was forced to sit out that tournament. Walsh played with another partner just for the training experience.

May tried to come back in late June to play at a grand slam event in Berlin, Germany. The team played one match and won, but May was in obvious pain. Knowing that her partner was so competitive that she would try to play through the injury, Walsh decided to take matters into her own hands. "Misty, I'm done," she told May. "I don't care what you say, I'm not playing." Although May was disappointed, she eventually agreed with Walsh's decision to withdraw from the tournament.

May ended up sitting out three more tournaments leading up to the Olympic Games in Athens, Greece. While May was out of action, Walsh paired up with Rachel Wacholder of France. They won the Marseilles Grand Slam, defeating the Brazilian team of Behar and Bede, and also won the Austrian Grand Slam, an event that Walsh had won the previous two years with May.

Winning the Gold in 2004

When Walsh and May traveled to Athens in August 2004, they were widely considered the most formidable beach volleyball duo of all time. They were expected to bring home an Olympic medal for the United States, although May's recent abdominal injury left a small shadow of doubt in the minds of some observers.

The Olympic beach volleyball venue in Athens became the site of a huge, raucous beach party during the women's tournament. More than 10,000 fans packed the grandstands, loud music pumped out of speakers, and bikini-clad dancing girls revved up the crowd. "It was so cool seeing 10,000 people at the venue screaming and having a great time," Walsh stated. "I think the Olympics will just keep propelling the popularity of our sport."

Walsh and May receiving their Olympic medals.

Walsh and May played their first Olympic match against Japan on August 15, Walsh's 26th birthday. Walsh capped the 43-minute contest with a dazzling spike. True to form, the American duo went on to dominate the remainder of the Olympic tournament, winning seven consecutive matches and never dropping a single game. In the semifinals, Walsh and May easily handled the other American team, Holly McPeak and Elaine Youngs. In the finals Walsh and May faced the Brazilian team of Shelda Bede and Adriana Behar. Bede and Behar had held the top ranking in the world standings five times and claimed the silver medal in Sydney. But Walsh and May disposed of the Brazilians in typically breezy fashion, winning the best of three series in two games, 21-17 and 21-11, to claim the first-ever gold medal for the United States in women's beach volleyball.

After scoring the final point and sealing the gold, Walsh and May jumped into each other's arms for an exuberant hug. They ended up falling over into the sand. Nicknamed the "horizontal hug," this spontaneous moment of celebration was replayed over and over on television news and sports programs. Some commentators found the sight of two women in bathing suits rolling around in the sand to be sexually suggestive. But Walsh and May dismissed this idea as ridiculous. "It was a moment of celebration and joy," Walsh explained. "I'd like to see what someone else would do after working for years for that moment. I'd like to see how they'd celebrate if they were in our shoes. Would they just slap hands and walk away? I don't think so. We were both so pumped." Not ashamed of their true affection for one another, Walsh and May held hands on the medal stand as the U.S. national anthem played.

Walsh ended up giving her gold medal to her parents, who were watching in the stands along with her brother, Marte. "This is for my entire family," she stated. "I hope they know how much they mean to me. Sports are such a lifestyle in my family." Her mother, Margie, had promised to get a tattoo if Kerri won a gold medal. "Be careful of what you promise your kids," she said afterward.

> *The Olympic beach volleyball venue in Athens became the site of a huge, raucous beach party during the women's tournament. More than 10,000 fans packed the grandstands, loud music pumped out of speakers, and bikini-clad dancing girls revved up the crowd. "It was so cool seeing 10,000 people at the venue screaming and having a great time," Walsh stated. "I think the Olympics will just keep propelling the popularity of our sport."*

Going Forward

Walsh and May have been called the best beach volleyball team ever to play the game. In addition, each player individually has been called the best ever by various sources. Three-time beach volleyball gold medalist Karch Kiraly noted that "Kerri combines the skills of a really small player with a player who's a lot taller. . . . That's why she's so good and that's why they're the best women's team ever."

At the beginning of their partnership, the duo were coached by May's father, Butch. Their coach at the Olympics was former top-tier beach player Dane Selznick, who calls them the "easiest team I've ever worked with. Kerri is in the game 150 percent of the time every second, and she shows it. Misty is more the cloak and dagger type. Kerri's clapping and dictating the action verbally to Misty. She's kind of the quarterback. Misty, she's all business." Together, the two players' strong all-around skills create a deadly combination.

Instead of resting on their laurels after the Olympics, Walsh and May were back in action on the AVP tour in September. The popularity they achieved in Athens has helped advance their sport, which is increasingly featured on American television networks. Some commentators have criticized the women's beach game, attributing its appeal to the fact that the players wear two-piece bathing suits. But Walsh rejects such criticism. "I don't feel objectified at all in what I do," she noted. "My uniform's a big part of what I do and I need it to be able to play well. It's very functional, and if I were out there playing in big baggy clothes, it wouldn't work. We wouldn't be as good as we were. And it's an intriguing part of the sport. We're all very athletic, we're all very fit. I don't think we're out there wearing skimpy suits, we're out there wearing sporty suits."

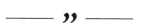

> "I'm the spastic one. I'm just really emotional. I have so much anxiety in me, and I don't know how to channel it. So it comes out like I'm a cheerleader, which is OK to an extent," Walsh acknowledged. "If I'm playing a match, I'm nervous and excited. My butterflies are out of control and my heart rate is out of control. I try to slow my energy down or slow my mind down and just breathe a lot."

Walsh and May practice together three to four times a week, and they also do individual workouts. Although they spend a great deal of time together practicing, traveling, and playing in tournaments, they have remained close friends. "We're good friends, but when we're on the road together, we're together 24/7, really and truly. So when times are bad, it's tough — you really have to work through your things — and when they're good, they're great," Walsh explained. "We have great chemistry. We've logged a lot of hours over the four years we've been playing together. We're different in some respects, but we're also very similar in others. We're both relentless. We're both competitive."

Of the two players, Walsh admits that she is by far the more emotional. "I'm the spastic one. I'm just really emotional. I have so much anxiety in me, and I don't know how to channel it. So it comes out like I'm a cheer-

leader, which is OK to an extent," she acknowledged. "If I'm playing a match, I'm nervous and excited. My butterflies are out of control and my heart rate is out of control. I try to slow my energy down or slow my mind down and just breathe a lot."

Between them, Walsh and May have earned over one million dollars in prize money. They have increased their earnings significantly through high-profile endorsement deals with Visa, Speedo, Gatorade, McDonald's, and other companies. They have appeared in television commercials and on a number of talk shows, thus providing exposure to the entire sport of beach volleyball. Walsh and May hope to continue playing together for many years to come.

HOME AND FAMILY

Walsh lives in Redondo Beach, California. She shares a home with her boyfriend, Casey Jennings, who also plays beach volleyball. In November 2004 Walsh served as a bridesmaid for May, who married Florida Marlins catcher Matt Treanor.

HOBBIES AND OTHER INTERESTS

Walsh enjoys music, and she listens to Sade and Dave Matthews to calm herself down before games. She also likes to read, and one of her favorite books is *The Alchemist* by Paulo Coelho.

HONORS AND AWARDS

Gatorade National High School Volleyball Player of the Year: 1995
First-Team NCAA All-American: 1996-99
NCAA Co-Player of the Year: 1999
FIVB World Tour Championship: 2002, 2003
AVP Best Offensive Player: 2003
AVP Most Valuable Player: 2003, 2004
AVP Team of the Year: 2003, 2004
Olympic Women's Beach Volleyball: 2004, gold medal (with Misty May)
U.S. Olympic Spirit Award: 2004
Team Sportswomen of the Year (Women's Sports Foundation): 2004
    (with Misty May)

FURTHER READING

Books

Who's Who in America, 2005

Periodicals

Atlanta Journal-Constitution, Aug. 25, 2004, p.D5
Chicago Sun-Times, Sep. 5, 2004, Section 3, p.10
Chicago Tribune, Sep. 15, 2004, p.C2
Las Vegas Review-Journal, Sep. 9, 2004, p.C2
New York Times, July 10, 2004, p.D5
Outside, Dec. 2004, p.86
San Diego Union-Tribune, June 10, 2004, p.D1
San Francisco Chronicle, Dec. 2, 1999, p.E3; June 13, 2004, p.C1
San Jose Mercury News, Mar. 21, 1996, p.D6; Dec. 21, 1996, p.D1; Aug. 25, 2004, p.A1
Sports Illustrated, June 7, 2004, p.Z8
USA Today, Dec. 18, 1996, p.C4; Sep. 27, 2000, p.E7; Aug. 13, 2004, p.C1; Aug. 16, 2004, p.D11; Aug. 25, 2005, p.D9

ADDRESS

Kerri Walsh
Association of Volleyball Professionals
6080 Center Drive, 6th Floor
Los Angeles, CA 90045

WORLD WIDE WEB SITES

http://www.kerriwalsh.com
http://www.usoc.org
http://www.avp.com
http://www.fivb.org

Photo and Illustration Credits

Gretchen Bleiler/Photos: Riccardo S. Savi/WireImage.com (p. 9); Alexandra Winkler/ Reuters (p. 11); AP/Wide World Photos (p. 14); Donald Miralle/Getty Images (p. 17).

Lynne Cox/Photos: AP/Wide World Photos (p. 20); Hulton Archive/Getty Images (p. 23); copyright © Bettmann/CORBIS (p. 25, 27); photo by Gabriella Miotto (p. 32); Allen J. Schaben/*Los Angeles Times* (p. 36). Cover: SWIMMING TO ANTARCTICA (Alfred A. Knopf) copyright © 2004 by Lynne Cox.

Daunte Culpepper/Photos: Jonathan Daniel/Getty Images (p. 38); Ted Kirk/Time Life Pictures/Getty Images (p. 42); Ezra O. Shaw/Getty Images (p. 45); AP/Wide World Photos (p. 47); Tom Mihalek/EPA/Landov (p. 50).

Julie Foudy/Photos: Lisa Blumenfeld/Getty Images (p. 54); Rod Searcey/Stanford Athletics (p. 57); AP/Wide World Photos (p. 61, 65); John Mottern/AFP/Getty Images (p. 63); Marcos Brindicci/Reuters/Landov (p. 68). Front cover: Richard Schulz/WireImage.com.

Laird Hamilton/Photos: copyright © Tony Friedkin/Sony Pictures Classics/ZUMA/ CORBIS (p. 71); Wareen Bolster/*Sports Illustrated* (p. 73, 75); copyright © Les Walker/ NewSport/CORBIS (p. 77); Tim McKenna/Dolphin Image Productions/CORBIS (p. 78); Robert Beck/*Sports Illustrated* (p. 81).

Betty Lennox/Photos: Jeff Reinking/NBAE/Getty Images (p. 85, front cover); AP/Wide World Photos (pp. 88, 91, 96); Jeff Vinnick/Getty Images (p. 94).

Michael Phelps/Photos: Stuart Hannagan/Getty Images (p. 100); Doug Pensinger/Getty Images (p. 103); Daneil Berehulak/FINA/Getty Images (p. 106, top); Mark J. Terrill/ Pool/Reuters/Landov (p. 106, middle); Chris Ivin/WireImage.com (p. 106, bottom); AP/Wide World Photos (p. 109, 114); David Gray/Reuters/Landov (p. 111). Front cover: MPS/WireImage.com.

Manny Ramirez/Photos: AP/Wide World Photos (p. 119); Tom G. Lynn/Time Life Pictures/Getty Images (p. 125); Brian Snyder/Reuters (p. 127); Jason Szenes/EPA/ Landov (p. 130-31); Mike Blake/Reuters/Landov (p. 132).

Vijay Singh/Photos: Stan Badz/PGA Tour/WireImage.com (p. 136); Ezra O. Shaw/Getty Images (p. 141); Craig Jones/Getty Images (p. 143); Tim Sloan/AFP/Getty Images (p. 146); Al Messerschmidt/WireImage.com (p. 149). Front cover: Chris Condon/PGA Tour/WireImage.com.

Kerri Walsh/Photos: Philippe Desmazes/AFP/Getty Images (p. 151, 157); Rod Searcey/ Stanford Athletics (p. 154); Ian Waldie/Getty Images (p. 160); AP/Wide World Photos (p. 163).

Cumulative General Index

This cumulative index includes names, occupations, nationalities, and ethnic and minority origins that pertain to all individuals profiled in *Biography Today* since the debut of the series in 1992.

For cumulative places of birth and birthday indexes, please see biographytoday.com.

169

For cumulative places of birth and birthday indexes, please see biographytoday.com.

For cumulative places of birth and birthday indexes, please see biographytoday.com.

For cumulative places of birth and birthday indexes, please see biographytoday.com.

For cumulative places of birth and birthday indexes, please see biographytoday.com.

For cumulative places of birth and birthday indexes, please see biographytoday.com.

For cumulative places of birth and birthday indexes, please see biographytoday.com.

For cumulative places of birth and birthday indexes, please see biographytoday.com.

187

For cumulative places of birth and birthday indexes, please see biographytoday.com.

For cumulative places of birth and birthday indexes, please see biographytoday.com.

For cumulative places of birth and birthday indexes, please see biographytoday.com.

For cumulative places of birth and birthday indexes, please see biographytoday.com.

193

For cumulative places of birth and birthday indexes, please see biographytoday.com.

For cumulative places of birth and birthday indexes, please see biographytoday.com.

For cumulative places of birth and birthday indexes, please see biographytoday.com.

207

For cumulative places of birth and birthday indexes, please see biographytoday.com.

Biography Today

General Series

"Biography Today **will be useful in elementary and middle school libraries and in public library children's collections where there is a need for biographies of current personalities. High schools serving reluctant readers may also want to consider a subscription."**
— *Booklist,* American Library Association

"Highly recommended for the young adult audience. Readers will delight in the accessible, energetic, tell-all style; teachers, librarians, and parents will welcome the clever format, intelligent and informative text. It should prove especially useful in motivating 'reluctant' readers or literate nonreaders."
— *MultiCultural Review*

"Written in a friendly, almost chatty tone, the profiles offer quick, objective information. While coverage of current figures makes *Biography Today* a useful reference tool, an appealing format and wide scope make it a fun resource to browse." — *School Library Journal*

"The best source for current information at a level kids can understand."
— Kelly Bryant, School Librarian, Carlton, OR

"Easy for kids to read. We love it! Don't want to be without it."
— Lynn McWhirter, School Librarian, Rockford, IL

*B*iography Today **General Series** includes a unique combination of current biographical profiles that teachers and librarians — and the readers themselves — tell us are most appealing. The **General Series** is available as a 3-issue subscription; hardcover annual cumulation; or subscription plus cumulation.

Within the **General Series**, your readers will find a variety of sketches about:

- Authors
- Musicians
- Political leaders
- Sports figures
- Movie actresses & actors
- Cartoonists
- Scientists
- Astronauts
- TV personalities
- and the movers & shakers in many other fields!

ONE-YEAR SUBSCRIPTION
- 3 softcover issues, 6" x 9"
- Published in January, April, and September
- 1-year subscription, $60
- 150 pages per issue
- 10 profiles per issue
- Contact sources for additional information
- Cumulative Names Index

HARDBOUND ANNUAL CUMULATION
- Sturdy 6" x 9" hardbound volume
- Published in December
- $62 per volume
- 450 pages per volume
- 30 profiles — includes all profiles found in softcover issues for that calendar year
- Cumulative General Index

SUBSCRIPTION AND CUMULATION COMBINATION
- $99 for 3 softcover issues plus the hardbound volume

For Cumulative General, Places of Birth, and Birthday Indexes, please see www.biographytoday.com.

Biography Today
Subject Series

For ages 9 and above

Expands and complements the General Series and targets specific subject areas ...

Our readers asked for it! They wanted more biographies, and the *Biography Today* **Subject Series** is our response to that demand. Now your readers can choose their special areas of interest and go on to read about their favorites in those fields. Priced at just $39 per volume, the following specific volumes are included in the *Biography Today* **Subject Series**:

- **Authors**
- **Business Leaders**
- **Performing Artists**
- **Scientists & Inventors**
- **Sports**

FEATURES AND FORMAT

- Sturdy 6" x 9" hardbound volumes
- Individual volumes, $39 each
- 200 pages per volume
- 10 profiles per volume — targets individuals within a specific subject area
- Contact sources for additional information
- Cumulative General Index

For Cumulative General, Places of Birth, and Birthday Indexes, please see www.biographytoday.com.

NOTE: There is *no duplication of entries* between the **General Series** of *Biography Today* and the **Subject Series**.

AUTHORS

"A useful tool for children's assignment needs." — *School Library Journal*

"The prose is workmanlike: report writers will find enough detail to begin sound investigations, and browsers are likely to find someone of interest." — *School Library Journal*

SCIENTISTS & INVENTORS

"The articles are readable, attractively laid out, and touch on important points that will suit assignment needs. Browsers will note the clear writing and interesting details." — *School Library Journal*

"The book is excellent for demonstrating that scientists are real people with widely diverse backgrounds and personal interests. The biographies are fascinating to read." — *The Science Teacher*

SPORTS

"This series should become a standard resource in libraries that serve intermediate students." — *School Library Journal*

Order Annual Sets of *Biography Today* and Save Up to 20% Off the Regular Price!

Now, you can save time and money by purchasing *Biography Today* in Annual Sets! Save up to 20% off the regular price and get every single biography we publish in a year. Billed upon publication of the first volume, subsequent volumes are shipped throughout the year upon publication. Keep your *Biography Today* library current and complete with Annual Sets!

Place a standing order for annual sets and receive an additional 10% off!

Regular price $239
2005 Annual Set $199
You Save $40

Biography Today 2005 Annual Set

7 volumes. 0-7808-0782-0. Annual set, $199. Includes:

2005 subscription (3 softcover issues);
2005 Hardbound Annual; Authors, Vol. 17;
Scientists & Inventors, Vol. 10; Sports, Vol. 13

Regular price $335
2004 Annual Set $268
You Save $67

Biography Today 2004 Annual Set

8 volumes. 0-7808-0731-6. Annual set, $268. Includes:

2004 Hardbound Annual; Authors, Vols. 15 and 16;
Business Leaders, Vol. 1; Performing Artists, Vol. 3;
Scientists & Inventors, Vol. 9;
Sports, Vols. 11 and 12

Regular price $335
2003 Annual Set $268
You Save $67

Biography Today 2003 Annual Set

8 volumes. 0-7808-0730-8. Annual set, $268. Includes:

2003 Hardbound Annual; Authors, Vols. 13 and 14;
Performing Artists, Vols. 1 and 2;
Scientists & Inventors, Vol. 8; Sports, Vols. 9 and 10

Regular price $297
2002 Annual Set $237
You Save $60

Biography Today 2002 Annual Set

7 volumes. 0-7808-0729-4. Annual set, $237. Includes:

2002 Hardbound Annual; Authors, Vols. 11 and 12;
Scientists & Inventors, Vols. 6 and 7;
Sports, Vols. 7 and 8